A History *of* St. George's

Catholicism in North Norwich 1896-2016

A History *of* St. George's

Catholicism in North Norwich 1896-2016

Fred Corbett

STEPHEN MORRIS

First published in 2016 by Stephen Morris
www.stephen-morris.co.uk
T: 0208 946 8705
E: smc@freeuk.com

ISBN 978-0-9930554-5-4

British Library Cataloguing-in-Publication Data
A catalogue record for this book is available from the British Library

Designed and produced by Stephen Morris, smc@freeuk.com www.stephen-morris.co.uk
Minion 11/13
Printed by Akcent Media

CONTENTS

Foreword

In 2016 St. George's Parish celebrates a golden jubilee: the fiftieth anniversary of the consecration of our beautiful church on Sprowston Road, a spiritual home to so many people in our large and thriving parish and the 'mother' church to our three communities of Sprowston, Hellesdon and Thorpe. 2016 marks another anniversary also: the 120th year since the raising of the parish back in 1896.

Many events have been planned in the parish for 2016, including liturgical celebrations and social get togethers. There has been a determined effort to shift the focus outward, to include our friends and neighbours in this part of the city and to attract as wide an audience as possible to come and celebrate with us.

It's significant that the first two events of our jubilee year include an ecumenical service of praise and worship of God and the launch of this book by Fred Corbett. The heart of our jubilee remains an act of thanksgiving to God for what has gone before and a desire to be ever more closely united as Christians as we go forward.

Fred's book, *A History of St. George's*, is the fruit of much labour but also of much love. He is not writing about some abstract, distant group of people who once did this and once did that. Fred writes with real affection about people still remembered with fondness among the parish; about people still here in the parish and still building our community. *A History of St. George's* is a family's story and told by one very much at the heart of that family.

Fred narrates the birth and building of the 'new' St. George's church, as people still call it even after 50 years. Importantly, he sets this building within the context of the growth of the wider parish and of the expansion of Catholicism within the north part of the city of Norwich and beyond. Fred's work paints a fascinating diary-like account of the working of the parish over 120 years, acknowledging it's ups and downs, and recognising the commitment and hard work of the people of the parish and their priests.

This book is an important piece of local history and also an important part of the heritage of St. George's as we move forward. It calls us to gratitude for what we have inherited as a parish in the twenty-first century and reminds us of the levels of commitment called for to keep our community alive and active. Central to all the activity and expansion and building work written about in this book is the reason for our parish and our parish church: a home in which we can come together to support one another and encounter Christ together; a place from which to offer God's love to others; a physical sign in brick and mortar of the living Church that dwells among the people of north Norwich and beyond.

Fr. Sean Connolly, Parish Priest
Spring 2016

Introduction

The Parish of St. George's Norwich

The Brick
The bricklayer laid a brick on the bed of cement.
Then with a precise stroke of his trowel spread another layer
And without a by-your-leave, laid on another brick.
The foundations grew visibly,
The building rose, tall and strong, to shelter men.

I thought, Lord, of that brick buried in the darkness at the base of the big building,
No one sees it, but it accomplishes its task, and the other bricks need it.
Lord, what difference whether I am on the roof-top or in the foundations of your building,
As long as I stand faithfully at the right place?

This wonderful short poem by Michel Quoist[1] reminds us that no matter where we are in the structure we all have a role, the whole is dependant on all the parts. It isn't just the most visible that are the most important. For a Parish that grew up around ancient brickfields, brick kilns and brick-makers (now really only visible in some local pub names), and for a book written to celebrate the 50th anniversary of the consecration of a brick building, Michel Quoist's poem is rather apt.

At the Solemn High Mass celebrating the Consecration of St. George's Church in 1966 The Rev. Michael Hazell said that

> a church is only a memorial in bricks and mortar to the life of the parish. The parishioners should be 'living stones', closely linked to one another through charity. They should be remembered for their actions rather than their buildings.

In 2012 a group of young people preparing for their Confirmation reflected on the meaning of the word 'parish', they wrote

> Parish means Christ's presence among men and women;
> Parish means a set of persons;
> Parish means a community in which Jesus Christ confirms the presence of God;
> The parish is a living part of the people of God.

So this history will tell the tale of how St. George's came to be built, but more importantly try to tell the tale of how Catholic Christianity has flourished in Norwich and in this parish over many more years.

The parish covers the whole of Norwich north of the River Wensum as it flows through the city and where it is next to the Cathedral Parish of St. John The Baptist. In the west it covers the area out through Catton and Hellesdon and abuts on to the Costessey Parish. To the east it covers all of The Heartsease area, Thorpe St. Andrew and out through Little Plumstead and Brundell on the River Yare, bordering on to the Great Yarmouth Parish. To the north the parish extends out through Sprowston, Spixworth and almost as far as Wroxham. In fact up until a reorganisation of the parishes in 2002 the Parish of St. George's included the beautiful church of St. Helens in Hoveton but that is now part of the North Walsham Parish.

It is a wonderful urban and rural area with much of beauty and interest within it. It includes ancient parish churches now centres of our sister Anglican parishes of;- Sprowston, Catton, Hellesdon, part of Drayton, Horsford, Horsham St. Faith, Spixworth, Crostwick, Rackheath, Little and Great Plumstead, Blofield, Witton, Strumpshaw, Brundell, Postwick, Thorpe St. Andrew and parts of The City Of Norwich. It is rich in historic sites of local and national interest, sites of natural beauty bordering on to the Norfolk Broads National Park, ancient and new communities as well as acres of open space and an interesting range of old and new businesses.

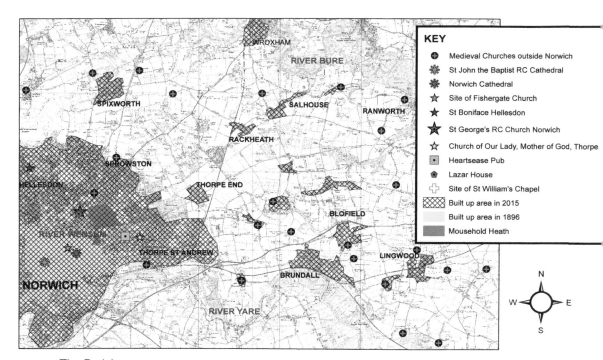

The Parish

Chapter 1

The Consecration and Dedication of St. George's, 1966

I'm sure most of us have had that experience of moving into a house or flat and arriving only to find the builders still finishing things off or previous tenants making the final repairs before handing over the keys. Well the story of our church started in similar vein. You wouldn't believe how tight things were.

For those of you that remember, the winter of 1964 was bitterly cold and we had freezing conditions from around Christmas to well into March. One of the coldest in living memory.

St. George's Church opened in Passion Week 1964, on Wednesday, 18 March. Last minute preparations were immense and frenetic: 50 men continued to work on the last three days before the opening – with the organ installed, tiles, flag-stones laid and tarmac laid and sacristy furnishings installed. The last workman finished just after 6pm on 18 March and at 6.30 p.m. the Solemn Blessing and Opening of the Church began with Solemn High Mass for a packed church.

The total cost was £76,500 plus £6,000 for the Hall which seems quite reason-able to us now but that was a challenging amount in those days. In 1966 the average house price was £3,840, petrol was 5 shillings (or 26 pence) a gallon. At the time of opening the debt was £33,000 and this was cleared by the early part of 1966. Real testimony to the way the Development Association was led and supported and to the great generosity of the parishioners of St. George's Parish. With the debt cleared the church could then be consecrated and this took place on Tuesday 24 May 1966.

The Consecration

Mass was celebrated by Rev. Anthony Roberts assisted by Rev. J. Smith and the Rev. W. Strain. The Consecration was carried out by Rt. Rev. T. Leo Parker (Bishop of Northampton) assisted by Rt. Rev. Joseph E. Rudderham (Bishop of Clifton) and Rt. Rev. Charles A. Grant (Bishop of Alinda, Auxiliary Bishop of Northamp-ton). The homily was given by Rev. Michael Hazell. In the previous week Fr. Roberts had received a letter from the Bishop confirming that the relics of martyrs made available for each altar to consecrate the church were to be *Sanctus Crecen-tius* (an old favourite) and *Sancta Benedicta* (a newcomer).

The programme for the consecration set out the details for the Consecration Mass. As the *Eastern Daily Press* reported at the time 'the two and a-half hour service began in warm sunshine' and the solemn joyful ceremony proceeded as follows: after a period of prayer before the relics the clergy with the Bishop processed to the main door where the congregation awaited outside. The Bishop then blessed the outside walls with Gregorian Water (water for health and clean-

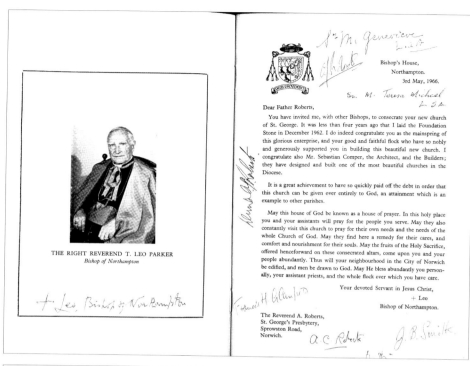

THE RIGHT REVEREND T. LEO PARKER
Bishop of Northampton

Bishop's House,
Northampton.
3rd May, 1966.

Dear Father Roberts,

You have invited me, with other Bishops, to consecrate your new church of St. George. It was less than four years ago that I laid the Foundation Stone in December 1962. I do indeed congratulate you as the mainspring of this glorious enterprise, and your good and faithful flock who have so nobly and generously supported you in building this beautiful new church. I congratulate also Mr. Sebastian Comper, the Architect, and the Builders; they have designed and built one of the most beautiful churches in the Diocese.

It is a great achievement to have so quickly paid off the debt in order that this church can be given over entirely to God, an attainment which is an example to other parishes.

May this house of God be known as a house of prayer. In this holy place you and your assistants will pray for the people you serve. May they also constantly visit this church to pray for their own needs and the needs of the whole Church of God. May they find here a remedy for their cares, and comfort and nourishment for their souls. May the fruits of the Holy Sacrifice, offered henceforward on these consecrated altars, come upon you and your people abundantly. Thus will your neighbourhood in the City of Norwich be edified, and men be drawn to God. May He bless abundantly you personally, your assistant priests, and the whole flock over which you have care.

Your devoted Servant in Jesus Christ,

+ Leo
Bishop of Northampton.

The Reverend A. Roberts,
St. George's Presbytery,
Sprowston Road,
Norwich.

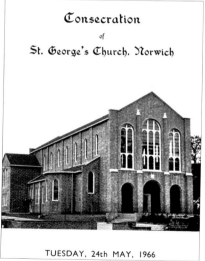

Consecration

of

St. George's Church. Norwich

TUESDAY, 24th MAY, 1966

'May they find here a remedy for their cares, and comfort and nourishment for their souls'.
The autographed Consecration programme from Tuesday, 24 May 1966, including a letter from Leo Parker, Bishop of Nothamptonshire, to Fr. Roberts

liness to which salt is added for food, ashes for repentance and wine for the generosity of God). The Bishop then knocked on the main door which was opened by the Deacon-Guard, and the Bishop, clergy and congregation moved in procession into the church. Then the Bishop sprinkled the inside walls with the Gregorian Water, praying that God would hallow the place and protect the faith of all who use the church, and to make it a place of refuge and joy. After that

Bishop Leo Parker and his assistants prepare for the blessing of the walls

The Bishop and assistants process into the church

The Bishop traces the Greek and Latin alphabets in the ashes of a 9-feet-long cross laid out on the floor in front of the Sanctuary gates

● The Bishop of Northampton, the Rt. Rev. T. Leo Parker, traces the Greek and Latin alphabets in a cross of ashes with his staff during the ceremony of S George's Roman Catholic Church, Sprowston, today.

Bishop Leo Parker and his assistants celebrate High Mass

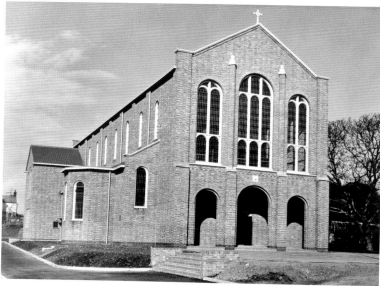

St. George's, 1964

the Altar was sprinkled tracing five crosses with the water to sanctify it.
The church was dedicated by tracing the Greek and Latin alphabets in the ashes of a 9-feet-long cross laid out on the floor in front of the Sanctuary gates and the relics were processed to their places of burial in cavities prepared in each Altar.

It was then time for the consecration of the Church and the Altar. Twelve crosses had been placed in the walls of the church. You can see these in the walls around the inside of the church, there are two at each end and four at each side of the church. The Bishop traced each cross in turn with Chrism saying:

One of twelve crosses in the walls blessed at the Consecration

Sr. Mary Paul (left) headmistress of St. Mary's Convent Lowestoft (now closed) and Sr. Catherine (right): two of three nuns who joined the celebration of the Consecration

> May this Church be made holy and consecrated in the name of the Father, and of the Son, and of the Holy Ghost, in honour of God, and in memory of St. George.

Finally the Altar itself was consecrated and prepared for the Solemn Mass of Dedication with the following words:

> O God, who unseen, upholdest all things and yet for the welfare of mankind showest visible signs of thy might, glorify this Church by the power of thy indwelling; and grant that all who gather here to seek thy mercy, in whatever trouble they call upon thee, may obtain thy blessing and thy comfort.

The dedication ended with the command to remember and celebrate this day each year as a Feast, so that generations yet unborn will come on this day and remember those who have struggled to build this church and to give it to God.

The first baptisms after the consecration were on the 29 May 1966 with baptisms for Karen Lesley Mary Galey from Meredith Road, Hellesdon and Jonathan James Ward of Firwood Close in Norwich.

So how did this great new church come about? The next chapter tells the story of the long battle to acquire a new place of worship in Norwich for the St. George's community. A story of many ups and downs, determination, negotiation, prayer, innovation and creativity and, of course, compromise.

WHAT WAS GOING ON IN *1966* IN THE WIDER WORLD?

23 March: Pope Paul VI and Arthur Michael Ramsey, the Archbishop of Canterbury, met in Rome – the first official meeting in 400 years between the Roman Catholic and Anglican Churches

6 April: Hoverlloyd inaugurated the first cross-Channel hovercraft service, from Ramsgate Harbour to Calais

7 April: United Kingdom asked the UN Security Council authority to use force to stop oil tankers violating the oil embargo against Rhodesia.

9 April: The 31-year-old Norwich City F.C. captain, Barry Butler, was killed in a car accident close to the church on Sprowston Road.

11 April: The Marquess of Bath, in conjunction with Jimmy Chipperfield, opened Longleat Safari Park, the first such drive-through park outside Africa.

15 April: *Time* magazine coined the phrase Swinging London.

30 April: Liverpool won the Football League First Division title for the second time in three seasons.

14 May: Everton defeated Sheffield Wednesday 3-2 in the FA Cup final at Wembley Stadium.

23 June: The Beatles went top of the British singles charts for the 10th time with *Paperback Writer*.

30 July: England defeated Germany to win the 1966 World Cup Final.

21 October: Aberfan disaster in South Wales. A slag heap destroyed twenty houses and a farm before going on to demolish virtually all of Pantglas Junior School; 144 people were killed, 116 of whom were children mostly between the ages of 7 and 10.

Chapter 2

The Development of the new Church

Trials and tribulations of growth
How St. George's came to be constructed in the 1960s

From 1896 until the 1960s the parish was centred on St. George's Fishergate, a delightful church on the edge of the old city of Norwich next to the River Wensum, and whose story follows in the next chapter.

By the beginning of the twentieth century Norwich was a sizeable and growing city but growth was significantly affected by both World Wars and the depression of the 1920s and 1930s. For all these trials, the most significant for St. George's as a parish was the post-war suburban growth of Norwich in the 1950s. St. George's became a large mixed urban, suburban and rural parish much as it is today. Thus the church at Fishergate was no longer big enough for the growing numbers wanting to attend Mass.

At the same time as demand for more space for the Catholic community was growing, the sad decline of the city's wonderful medieval churches was taking place. From 1948 and for the next ten years or so, the *Eastern Daily Press* was full of correspondence and reports concerning what to do with churches that were becoming redundant to requirements. This was initiated by concerns raised about the proposed demolition of St. Simon and St. Jude's Church in Elm Hill. The debate is captured well in the extracts from the local Norwich newspapers (*see over*).

The debate included strong representations from the Catholic Community to take over the church for their use. Sadly these discussions and negotiations, which went on throughout most of the 1950s, came to nothing.

While all the debate about churches went on for several years the growing Catholic community continued to be served by Fr. Kevin Jones. People were prepared for and received the sacraments, the community spirit grew in the austere environment following World War Two and during the Cold War years of the late 1940s and 1950s.

With great foresight and energy the people of the parish took a major step in controlling their own future as a worshipping community. Under the leadership of Fr. Jones and with the energy of Mr. Paul Jarvis, the Development Association was created in 1953 to raise funds for future developments on the acquired sites, whether church or school.

The fundraising efforts became a major focus for the whole parish and caught the imagination of people across the whole city and beyond. The funds raised were a remarkable testimony to the energy in the parish and all of this starting in

The Norfolk News
Weekly Press

Tel.: Norwich 23231 (6 lines)

SATURDAY, MAY 1, 1948

Shocking

THE recent statement about the Norwich church of SS. Simon and Jude that "it has been left to the Church Commissioners, in whom the site is vested, to arrange for its demolition after the removal of its ancient monuments," is one of the most shocking pronouncements on an ancient building that we remember to have read, and we are relieved to hear that Canon C. C. Lanchester, Rural Dean of Norwich, has since said that "if the Corporation were able to make use of the building. I am sure that the ecclesiastical authorities would be only too pleased." It will be readily agreed that the first call on the Church's money in Norwich is for the provision of places of worship on the new housing estates and that generally the spiritual needs of its communicants must come first. But the preservation of our medieval churches is a trust laid on this generation of which it cannot divest itself, and if the Church is not able to discharge that trust it must be prepared to delegate it to those who can.

Unwanted Churches

Sir—There will, I feel, be general sympathy for the Church of England in its problem of church redundancy, but it seems a pity to put a church to secular use when there are other religious communities in Norwich who could put them to the use for which they were originally built.

As Mr. Bulmer-Thomas remarked at the recent conference, reported in your columns—alluding to the Church of Saint Edmund, Fishergate — "no Christian can contemplate it without some feeling of shame." No "unwanted" church can be contemplated without a feeling of shame, yet just across the road from St. Edmunds a sizeable congregation of Norwich people are obliged, by force of circumstances, to make do for the worship of God with a shoddy converted schoolroom.

Can we then, in view of this situation, assume that a church is unwanted simply because it is redundent to one particular religious body in the city?—
Yours faithfully,
P. W. JARVIS.
Old Catton.

'The preserevation of our medieval churches is a trust laid on this generation': *Eastern Daily Press* 1 May 1948

'No unwanted Church can be contemplated without a feeling of shame': Paul Jarvis was a well-known and active parishioner. *EDP*

those austere, post-war years.

While planning for a new church went on, the parish continued to grow and the church was the focal point for many key times in people's lives. Chapter 4 picks up on life during this time in the parish, but for now we need to understand the challenging story about the building of the parish church.

In 1956 a further conference was held in London to explore the issues related to the large number of so-called redundant churches in cities like Norwich. Again the *Eastern Daily Press* for May 1956 contained extensive correspondence on the issue and the transfer of at least one church to the Roman Catholic community seemed to hold much favour. Despite the good wishes of many in the Anglican Church, no way could be found at that stage for such a transfer of use and eventually planning permission was sought for the new church on the Sprowston Road.

Just near the church is Hoopers Lane, the Showmen's Guild site. The Guild had a few sites situated around Norwich, required for storing their rides and equipment and for somewhere to live between fairs. Further up the road heading

The early sale of fundraising tickets – somewhat different to the National Lottery we are used to now

A Fishergate wedding: Ralph and Jean Daynes, 24 July 1954

away from the city is Windmill Road, the site of the famous post-mill, mill buildings and the mill house. This area was the site of the last of Sprowston's many brickyards. It closed in the 1950's, most of the other brickyards closed in the 1930's.

Along Sprowston Road you can see some attractive Victorian terraces on both sides of the road. In the early part of the twentieth century some were demolished, mainly on the opposite side to the church, to make way for new roads and the old Blyth Jex School. Many of the houses were originally the homes of shoe workers and brick makers who worked in Norwich and in the brick-making businesses prevalent in the area. The only remaining link to that history is in the bricks of

THE REST OF THE WORLD IN 1964

University of East Anglia took in its first students in buildings in Cathedral Close.

5 January: In the first meeting between leaders of the Roman Catholic and Orthodox churches since the 15th century, Pope Paul VI and Patriarch Athenagoras I met in Jerusalem.

23 January: Pope Paul VI instituted the World Day of Prayer for Vocations. It is being observed up to now. It is celebrated every Fourth Sunday of Easter also known as Good Shepherd Sunday.

6 February: The British and French governments agreed a deal for the construction of a Channel Tunnel.

10 March: The Queen gave birth to her fourth child, Prince Edward.

19 March: The government announced plans to build three new towns in South East England to act as overspill for overpopulated London. One of these around the village of Milton Keynes in north Buckinghamshire.

28 March: Pirate radio station Radio Caroline began broadcasting.

30 March: Violent disturbances between Mods and Rockers at Clacton beach.

9 April: Labour won the first elections to the Greater London Council.

16 April: Seven of the Great Train Robbers were sentenced to 30 years each for their role in the 1963 robbery.

18 April: Liverpool won the Football League First Division for the sixth time.

21 April: BBC Two began scheduled broadcasting.

2 May: West Ham United won the FA Cup for the first time in their history, beating Preston North End 3-2 at Wembley Stadium.

The Prime Minister Sir Alec Douglas-Home till 16 October and Harold Wilson From 16 October 1964.

THE FOLLOWING INVENTIONS HELPED CHANGE OUR LIVES IN DIFFERENT WAYS

BASIC (Beginners' All-purpose Symbolic Instruction Code), an easy-to-learn high-level. computer programming language was introduced.

Sony introduced the first VCR Home Video Recorder.

The computer mouse was invented by Douglas Engelbart in the USA.

Bubble Wrap was invented in the USA by Marc A Chavannes.

AND OTHER EVENTS IN POPULAR CULTURE

Sidney Poitier became the first black actor to win the best actor Oscar.

The Rolling Stones released their debut album, 'The Rolling Stones'.

The Beatles had 13 singles in Billboard's Hot 100.

Hasbro launched G.I. Joe, an action figure to join the Barbie Doll.

Roald Dahl's *Charlie and the Chocolate Factory* was published.

Top of the Pops premiered on BBC television.

Sprowston Road

the houses, and the Brickmakers Arms at the northern end of Sprowston Road.

Initial plans were turned down but after much hard and creative work by the architect, amendments were made and eventually in September 1961 the plans were approved and the Bill of Quantities prepared; contractors were invited to tender.

On Sunday 10 June 1962 Fr. Roberts was able to announce that the Bishop had accepted the tender from Messrs R.G. Carter at the sum of £47,575 and work was scheduled to commence on 25 June and due for completion on 14 December 1963. At that time the Development Fund was £27,300.

In preparation for the building, parishioners had helped clear parts of the site and the work was completed by a group of Irish men working in the city who financed and levelled the site.

In July 1962 Fr. Roberts went on retreat to Cambridge and was interrupted on day three with a frantic telephone call from the presbytery – 'The contractors can find no bottom to the subsoil; engineers have been called in and piling will be necessary; the architect wants to move the position of the church some forty feet nearer the house!'

Subsequent meetings confirmed that the church did not need to be moved but that the piling was essential, especially in the area where the Sacristy was to be built. The cost … an estimated additional £3,000! Piling of 30 feet was needed at the weakest end and 10 to 15-foot piles for all of the rest.

Early surveys had not revealed the need for this but several people with local knowledge showed that local wisdom can sometimes be more valuable than technology and that indeed the site was a disused pit related to brick making and that there were probably tunnels underneath.

The work commenced and eventually piles of 60-98 feet were needed before any solid bottom was found. In total 91 piles were sunk at an additional cost of some £9,000. The first brick was laid on 5 October 1962.

A parishioner, Linda Iaccarino (neé Hannant) remembers the building of the church at that time:

As a school leaver in 1962 and just starting out in the world of work, I commuted from my home into Norwich passing what was an empty space on Sprowston Road. Then the builders moved in and slowly the site started to take shape. I did not know that it was to be a church, as I had not seen or heard anything of the plans. Eventually when the windows went in it was obvious. Sitting on the top deck of the bus every day it was easy to see St. George's rise from the ground, brick by brick, never thinking that one day I would be married there as I was, at that time, a member of the Church of England. Having met my future husband shortly after the church was consecrated, he being an Italian Catholic, it was to become his local church. When we became engaged I started coming to Mass with him. I decided to convert and started attending weekly meetings of instruction with Fr. John Smith in 1970 – 71, and was baptised into the Catholic Faith in 1971 and I have been a parishioner of St. George's ever since.

On 22 December 1962, the Bishop of Northampton laid the foundation stone.

Laying the Foundation Stone, 22 December 1962

1963 started with a bitterly cold winter, one of the coldest on record. Building work was delayed and most of the men were laid off over the early months but by the summer the roof trusses were in place and in September the roofing commenced.

February 19 1963 saw the inauguration of the parish's own Scout group. This was started by Fr. Anthony Roberts and became known as the 17th Norwich (St. George's). It is still a vibrant group and celebrated its 50th anniversary on 24 February 2013 with a special Mass and reception.

At that time a detailed house-to-house survey across the whole of Norwich North, visiting 32,000 homes, revealed 1,132 Catholic homes with an estimated Catholic population of about 3,000.

Laying the Foundation
Stone, 22 December 1962

'The bulk of the money
came from the sixpences
and shillings of ordinary
people.'

A sixpenny-ticket for the
Fishergate fundraising
efforts

FISHERGATE FUND-RAISER

PRICE 6d.
Ticket No. **A** 58

ST. GEORGE
FISHERGATE
PAROCHIAL
DEVELOPMENT
ASSOCIATION

FIRST NUMBER

Contestants select
any two numbers
from 1 to 50.
Licensed under the
Small Lotteries &
Gaming Act 1956.

PROMOTER
P. W. JARVIS
91 N. WALSHAM RD.
OLD CATTON
NORWICH

SECOND NUMBER

All claims to be
made within 14 days
of Draw.
Torn or defaced
tickets will be dis-
qualified.

Modern Press, 42/44 Bethel Street, Norwich

RAFFLE

A five-penny Turniptop
ticket with a £100
'Saturday Special' and a
£25 'Wednesday
Winner' – a lot of
money for the lucky
holders

"Turniptop" (Crosswords)
Tickets 5p Each
ST. GEORGE
DEVELOPMENT
ASSOCIATION
NORWICH

Reg. under B. G. & L. Act. 1963 (Sec. 45)
Promoter: P. W. Jarvis
c/o 223 Sprowston Road, Norwich

Monday to Saturday
Week 513 Aug 13-18 1973

£265 Weekly

£12.50 Each Day
Mon Tue Thur Fri

£25 'Wednesday Winner'
£100 'Saturday Special'

to holder of ticket bearing Initial Letters
of each of the FIRST THREE Crossword
SOLUTIONS in the Eastern Evening News

The front elevation for St. George's on the cover of *This Parish*, 1963

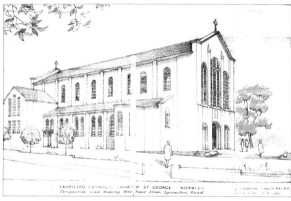

Architect drawings, 12 May 1961: view from the west

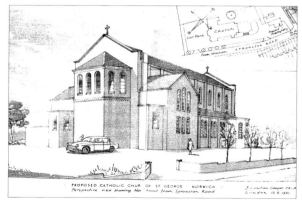

Architect drawings, 12 May 1961: view from the north

The Altar as it was on handover in 1964, before the changes resulting from the Second Vatican Council

The view from the Altar on handover and before the Second Vatican Council

The plans for the new church and first artist impressions were published in the *This is Your Parish* bulletin in 1963.

The parish worked hard to raise the funds through 'Turniptops', the drive of Mr. Paul Jarvis and the generosity of the parishioners. Paul was later presented with the Bene Merenti Medal in recognition of 20 years as promoter of the scheme that helped the parish build its churches and halls. When the fundraising scheme ended in 1980 it had raised about £0.5 million, ensuring all our buildings were debt-free and paying out lots of prize money in a pre-lottery time.

The building takes shape
The building of the church tried to ensure that it made a good contribution to the local economy. Besides the main builder, R.G. Carter of Drayton, the other principal contributors were the local firms of Mann Egerton Ltd. (seating), the Miller Organ Company and Eastern Electricity Board (under-floor heating and electrical fitting). The Altar furnishings, however, came from Vanpoulles of London and John Smythe of Dublin.

The time when St. George's Church was being planned and built co-incided with the Second Vatican Council: *Concilium Oecumenicum Vaticanum Secundum* (known as Vatican II) – the twenty-first Ecumenical Council of the Catholic Church and the second to be held at Saint Peter's Basilica in the Vatican. The council formally opened under Pope John XXIII on 11 October 1962 and closed under Pope Paul VI on the Feast of the Immaculate Conception in 1965. The original design of the church was based on approaches to liturgy and lay partic-ipation which predated Vatican II.

Pope John XXIII set the tone when opening the Council:

> The Church should never depart from the sacred treasure of truth inherited from the Fathers. But at the same time she must ever look to the present, to the new conditions and the new forms of life introduced into the modern world.[1]

Subsequently changes were made to the interior of the church to meet the outcomes of Vatican II. If you look carefully at these pictures (opposite) you can see changes to the design emanating from Vatican II's Four Constitutions – *Sacro-sanctum Concilium* (Constitution on the Sacred Liturgy) – which sought to increase participation in the liturgy. Thus the altar was turned to face the congre-gation, (and lay Eucharistic ministers and ministers of the word introduced) and barriers removed between the clergy and the congregation. Instead of Latin the vernacular language was permitted and encouraged.

The font was transferred from the old St. George's Church at Fishergate and initially placed in what is now the Holy Family Chapel. It was subsequently moved to its current, more prominent position just inside the main entrance.

Last minute delays in completion were caused by shortage of floor tiles, late arrival of the window glazing and a shortage of labour! Despite the delays St. George's Church opened in Passion Week 1964 on Wednesday 18 March.

The view to the Altar at handover

The view today, with the altar turned to face the congregation and with the altar rail removed

The Eastern Daily Press carried a full page on the 'New Roman Catholic Church'. [2]

In a short essay called – 'Getting Over the Style' – Fr. Roberts captured some of the debate of the time about the appearance of the church – He put it like this:

There was no lack of suggestions and contributions including sketches and models. One view was that it should evolve from its function with a centre piece altar, an oval or polygon or fan and in one suggestion the ground floor would be offices, community centre etc. But the majority 'voice' of the time was for a more traditional design – the new church was 'to look like a church', but what was that to mean? Little had really changed in church design over the centuries and it wasn't until the latter half of the 18th C that Catholics were able to build some new churches again, and the first two in

The Baptistery font rescued from Fishergate

The same font in its new location

Norwich, St. Swithin's and John the Baptist Maddermarket were built so as to attract as little attention as possible and therefore their external appearance was as unpretentious as possible. The Jesuit Chapel followed a continental, classical form. The new (later Cathedral) Church of St. John was pure Early English of George Gilbert Scott. These were the latter days of what was known as the Gothic Revival, and one of the leading exponents was Sir Ninian Comper. Examples of his style of restoration can be seen at Eye and at Wymondham Abbey.

The architectural work of his son Sebastian found much favour with the Bishop of Northampton – Bishop Leo Parker and he used Comper extensively for the design of diocesan churches. On gaining the commission for St. George's, Comper asked – "What style?" – Plans emerged for a generally Romansque style. The Bishop's Committee

The Church opening during Passion Week, March 1964. Msg. Leo Parker blesses the building

agreed but it was turned down by the city planners. Suggestions to 'modernise' its appearance seemed best to appease the local requirements but the architect said he would resign rather than employ a 'modern' style. Some changes were made but essentially Comper's design won through in what is said to be Comper's mixture style.

The West Window is Perpendicular in proportion but all the window arches are semi-circular. One architect has said that there are six different styles in the church.

On opening Bishop Parker described it as a 'glorious enterprise' and congratulated the team on designing and building one of the most beautiful churches in the Diocese. *The TV Times* called it 'The Church that Love Built' and described it as handsome, 'a landmark on the outskirts of Norwich'. The *The Eastern Daily Press* described it as 'positively beautiful' and paid tribute to the parish community in raising the necessary funds.

St. George's was built on the eve of Vatican II. Given another year or so the directives given might have been entirely different; for the Council's deliberations were to update the entire Roman Liturgy to a degree quite unforeseen in some episcopal circles. Within a short space of time the entire sanctuary area had to be completely re-orientated and the 'generous laity' had once again to dig into its pocket.

The first wedding and baptisms

The first wedding in the new St. George's Church was on Saturday the 21 March 1964 between William Charles Chadwick Howard of Spixworth Road and Diane Leslie Preece of Gertrude Road. The best man was Paul Howard and the Brides-maids were Miss Christine Preece (sister of the bride) Miss Valerie Hood (cousin of the bride) and Miss Janet Howard (sister of the bridegroom).

Thankfully the church was ready, though the front door was not finished, and though it was a cold, wet day photographs were taken. Fr. Roberts presided and

'Traditional style with low cost' – with seating for 450 in the centre of a big parish.
Eastern Daily Press, 19 March 1964

The very first wedding in the new church, between William Howard and Diane Preece: 21 March 1964

there was even the first confetti!

The first baptisms took place were on the 22 March. The honour fell to Steven John Gowing of Aylsham Road and Michael Graham Packer.

One of the parishioners, Frances Taylor, remembers aspects of parish life in those early days:

> I was one of the children that made their 'First Holy Communion' in the new church the year it opened. There was no hall for our 'communion breakfast' so we had our breakfast in what, to me as a child, seemed an enormous tent.

> The 'Turniptop' fundraiser scheme was famous all over Norwich (my future father-in-law bought these even though he's not a Catholic but because somebody on his road was selling them) at Fishergate, I remember Mrs. Wheeler used to sell them after Mass. I remember too, there was a group of 3 or 4 Irish men who we used to call the 'last in first out' blokes, you can work out why!

> I also remember there was a chap from Anglia TV who came to Mass (Bob Wellings I

'Peep from the Top': the Heartsease Estate. *Eastern Daily
Press*

think) who impressed me as I heard him ask for change from the collection basket for
the note he was putting in! Fishergate was also used to seeing a number of Norwich
City football stars: Terry Allcock and Kevin Keelan are two I remember well.

St. George's and St. John's used to combine to hire St. Andrew's Hall for a bazaar in
aid of both churches and I always remember the Valori family used to have a stall, I
seem to recall a large beautifully dressed doll as a prize laid out on their stall. The joint
churches' bazaar was a big social event for all the families in Norwich.

As I got older the big event was the St. George's joint Guide and Scout camp. I thor-
oughly enjoyed these and can't help thinking that we were more adventurous because
we had the boys with us rather than just Guides.

When St. George's opened the construction of the Heartsease Estate was well
underway. The *Eastern Daily Press* carried the headline 'Peep from the Top'.
Eleven storeys up and one member of the party – from the Council's Housing
Committee and City Architect's department – couldn't resist a peep over the wall
to see the view.

In January 1965 the new Parish Hall was fully operational and by Easter that
year the Fishergate Clubroom was restored after a fire and became the Headquar-
ters for the Scouts, Guides, Cubs and Brownies.

CHURCH THAT LOVE BUILT

by VICTOR EDWARDS

St. George's. "It's the apple of my eye," says the parish priest

THREE or four summers ago, if there was a fete going on in Norwich with some soberly attired clerical gentlemen around, you could make a private bet with yourself—and win it—that the function was in aid of the St. George's Roman Catholic church building fund.

All that is over now. The handsome, brick-built church that cost £76,500 is a landmark on the outskirts of Norwich.

And on Sunday morning, for the first time, Anglia Television will be transmitting *Sung Mass* from there. The assistant priest, Father John Smith, will offer Mass, and Father Anthony Roberts, the Parish Priest, will conduct the choir.

St. George's is a local church in the truest sense of the word. For eight years the driving force behind the energetic collection of money for its building came from Father Roberts. "St. George's," he agreed with a smile, "is the apple of my eye."

The church stands today as an example of the effort of local people, the amount of their own time they put into fund raising, and the generous way they dipped into their own pockets to get the money together.

Father Roberts told me there were a few small legacies. But the bulk of the money came from the sixpences and shillings of ordinary people.

For instance, one group of Irishmen in Norwich got together and paid for the hire of a bulldozer to level and clear the site.

Father Roberts has good stories to tell of the culmination of eight years' work when on the opening day of the new church—March 18, 1964—the Bishop of Northampton, the Rt. Rev. Leo Parker, was due to pronounce the solemn blessing at 6.30 p.m.

"At well after 6 p.m. the last workmen were gathering up their tools and beating a hasty retreat," he said. In fact, the congregation were taking their places while a workman was fixing the last floor tile. That's how close it was.

When the building began £43,500 had been saved. Something of the local support St. George's has enjoyed can be judged by the fact that the outstanding £33,000 has already been cleared.

Although the transmission of Sunday's service will be something of an occasion—the newest church in nothing special is being. Father Roberts told will be our normal Sunday Mass."

ANGLIA PLAY IT RIGHT

WHAT sort of plays do you like? The Independent Television Authority have been finding out in a special inquiry on play viewing. Some interesting points are made in their annual report.

You like history, crime, comedy and family situations. You like plenty of action and a satisfactory ending. You don't care at all for plays that feature sex and violence or those that leave you "in the air."

Special mention is made in the report of two of plays which are descr "unusual." They were election of a Pope, and bye Johnnie, about the poli campaign in Wor One.

The report also re "the continuing invent and vitality" existing regions. In this cor picks out, among oth Anglia Television ser Invaders in which Bri nell examined the in future of the East of E

'St. George's is the apple of my eye'.
A fitting tribute in the *TV Times*, 15 December 1965

Mr Bully, having been retired from business for some years had stepped down as organist as this new instrument, the Miller organ, might prove to be too 'big a beast' for him to control. The parish was indeed most fortunate to obtain, much due to Father Roberts's skills of persuasion, the regular services of Geoffrey Laycock, the senior music tutor at Keswick College south of Norwich, as organist and assistant choir master.

The above page from the *TV Times* of 15 December 1965 summarises the excitement and pride the whole community had at the time for all the work done in creating this new church for Norwich.

Chapter 3

From Chapels in the City to St. George's Fishergate

The early development of our Parish, 1896 to 1948

To me the only way to understand the story of the development of the parish up to the building of the new St. George's is to dip into some of the earlier history of Catholic worship in England and especially in this area. It is a story of prayer and great hope as well as tenacity and humility.

The historic background to the development of Catholic Parishes in Norwich
We can't underplay how difficult life had become for the Catholic community in England during the Reformation, from 1517 to 1648. In effect the Catholic community went underground from 1559 under Elizabeth I, for to be a Catholic brought with it the likelihood of being accused of being a traitor. Other than a three-year period under James II (1685-1688) the Church remained illegal in England for the next 230 years until it was legalised in 1791. Faith was kept alive by many committed and brave people supported by hard-working missionary priests, and the activities in particular of country house chapels such as that at Oxburgh, Costessey and Thorpe Halls. The 1791 Roman Catholic Relief Act meant that to be a Catholic was no longer illegal and treasonable; this was followed by the 1829 Act of Emancipation when Catholics received the right to vote, become a Member of Parliament and take part in government.

In Norwich there was a discreet Catholic Chapel, St. John the Baptist in Maddermarket where Mass was celebrated between 1794 and 1896. This is now the beautiful Maddermarket Theatre and you can still sense the features of the chapel when you are in the theatre. The Maddermarket brochure says

> Built in 1794 as a Roman Catholic Chapel, the premises were subsequently used as a grocery warehouse, the Salvation Army Young People's Hall, and as a general store. In 1921 it was converted, thanks to the work and imagination of Walter Nugent Bligh Monck (1878 – 1958) who had formed the Guild of Norwich Players in 1911. Monck was originally unimpressed by the dreary looking building but when inside he suddenly heard his own speaking voice ringing clearly around the building. The old Chapel's barrel roof appeared to boast the same acoustic properties as the Sistine Chapel upon which it was based. The exceptional sound persuaded Monck to purchase the building and so one of Norwich's wonderful cultural gems was born. Over the years in the theatre those working there have reported many sightings of a priest, a figure in black, a hooded figure in prayer and the smell of fresh incense.[1]

The Roman Catholic Chapel of St.
John The Baptist in 1893.In 1921 it
became the Maddermarket Theatre

St. John The Baptist

St. John The Baptist as the
Maddergate Theatre

The City's first purpose-built Roman Catholic Church, on Willow Lane. Later a primary school

When you visit this wonderful small theatre you can't help but be drawn into the atmosphere of its previous use no matter how wonderful or engaging the performance at the time.

The Old Chapel situated at the top of Willow Lane, off St. Giles Street in Norwich, was the first purpose-built Roman Catholic Church in the city, built in 1827-28 on land purchased by the Jesuits. J.T. Patience designed the building with a grand Palladian frontage. The Chapel was dedicated to Saints Peter and Paul and became known as the Holy Apostles Jesuit Chapel. Pevsner remarked that it is interesting that Patience chose an established Non-Conformist design for a Catholic Chapel. The building is built of grey brick with stucco details. It has a simple, dignified three-bay frontage with a central portico on paired Ionic columns and pilasters.[2] Patience also designed the Friends Meeting House in Upper Goat Lane.

Willow Lane also became a primary school familiar to many parishioners. Veronica Short remembers life at Willow Lane in the early 1960s:

> Before PE lessons the teacher would get a large bag of plimsolls and would throw them to you and you had to find a pair that fitted! I also remember being thrown toffees over the walls by factory workers next door. I don`t think I ever got one, though, as I didn't run fast enough! I also remember my dad appearing on the school playground with sweets for me.

Despite Emancipation there was a continuing, sometimes bitter, debate about the role of Catholicism in England. A pamphlet published in East Anglia called *A Discharge of Grape Shot against Authorities* sought to prove that the church of Rome, both in doctrine and practice, prohibited the reading of Holy Scripture. It was written by the late Rev. T.D. Atkinson, Fellow of Queens College Cambridge and then curate of St. Mary's Thetford. [3]

By 1850 some Catholics held very important social and political positions and one such person who had significant local influence was Henry Fitzalan-Howard who did a great deal to promote the Catholic cause amongst the ruling classes. His influence built on the work of families such as the Jerninghams of Costessey Hall, who did much to support the local Catholic community during the very difficult period of Catholic oppression pre-1791.

On 29 September 1850 by Letters Apostolic issued by Pope Pius IX (1792-1878), the English Hierarchy was restored, and the Diocese of Northampton came into being, covering an area from Slough through Buckinghamshire, Bedfordshire and Northamptonshire, Norfolk, Suffolk and Cambridgeshire. At the time of the 1851 Census of Religious Worship, perhaps one-in-three of all English people attended an Anglican Church service on a Sunday. Many others were drawn to the non-conformist chapels, especially in East Anglia. The Catholic Church barely registered on the radar of the 1851 census, especially in Norfolk and Suffolk.

With the re-establishment of the Church hierarchy in England and Wales there was a College of Bishops, led by the Archbishop of Westminster, each bishop having his own diocese. Because there were far fewer Catholics, the Catholic dioceses were much larger and Norwich was in the vast Diocese of Northampton. The Catholic Dioceses were chosen so that no city which already had an Anglican cathedral would be given a Catholic one, so as not to stir up anti-Catholic feeling. The new cathedrals were in places of significance to Church history, such as Southwark and Westminster, Leeds and Middlesbrough, Salford and Clifton.

The dioceses were carved up into Catholic parishes, again overlaying the Anglican ones, and again much bigger than their pre-Reformation counterparts. Whereas fifteenth-century Norwich had perhaps 36 Catholic parishes, there was now just one.

The middle of the nineteenth century was a time of change in Norwich as in most of Britain. In 1856 the New Colman's Mustard works opened at Carrow Road. This became world famous and represents an important aspect of the City's employment and wealth through the food and related products industries. Notre Dame High School for Girls was established in 1865 by the Sisters of Notre Dame and has been at the heart of Catholic education in Norfolk for over 150 years. Many of the senior staff at Notre Dame have played a prominent role in the parish over the years.

By 1870, the Holy Apostles Parish had a community of about 1,200 Catholics, and a further town-centre church followed in Fishergate Street. At that time Norwich was a staunchly Protestant town, uncomfortable with the ritualist movement within the Church of England, and barely tolerating the increasing Catholic presence within its midst.

The industrialisation of England led to the emergence, in the nineteenth century, of a large, urban, mainly poor, Catholic population. This was due, in part, to the large number of Irish immigrants following the shameful period of

'I wished to build a church as a thank-offering to God': Henry Fitzalan Howard, the 15th Duke of Norfolk

the Irish Famine in the mid 1800s. This change in the Catholic population sat ill-at-ease with the country house-led Catholicism of previous generations, but it was often the philanthropy of the landed Catholics which enabled the Catholic Church in urban areas to thrive. In the 1890s, Our Lady and the English Martyrs, a vast building, was opened in Cambridge. It had been erected thanks to the fortunes of Mrs. Lyne-Stephens of Lynford in Norfolk, and was one of the largest churches built in England in the nineteenth century. It was clear that if, as seemed likely, the Diocese of Northampton was one day split into two smaller dioceses, the Cambridge church would be ideal as the Cathedral of the new eastern diocese. Cambridge, after all, had no Anglican cathedral, while Norwich did. All over England, the Catholic communities were becoming more confident. Larger and larger churches were being erected. And yet, the mood seemed not to have affected Norwich, with its two small Catholic chapels.

However, one significant fact influenced the development of the Church in Norwich. The leading Catholic family of England then was that of the Dukes of Norfolk. The Duke of the day had been very generous with his money towards the building of the Cathedral at Southwark, and was responsible for the building of two great churches at Arundel and Sheffield, two places where the family had great influence. Norwich became his third great church.

On 2 July 1872 a Roman Catholic priest, Edmund Costello, died in Norwich after working amongst the poor in a smallpox epidemic in which 30 people per day were dying. In 1875, the Catholic Bishop of Northampton estimated that his entire flock in seven counties numbered just over 6,000. By 1880, with their mission accomplished, the Jesuits were preparing to leave Norwich. They then withdrew from Holy Apostles, which became a secular Mission in parallel with St. John's Maddermarket Catholic Chapel.

In 1877, Henry Fitzalan Howard, the 15th Duke of Norfolk, married. In 1892 he wrote a letter to the Mayor of Norwich, remembering the occasion.

> When, shortly after my most happy marriage, I wished to build a church as a thank-offering to God, many places were suggested to me. Bearing in mind the title that I hold, I decided to build this church in Norwich, the chief city of Norfolk.

A site had been purchased in Coslany, but before any clearance began, the 1827 city gaol came onto the market. This was also bought, and in 1881 the buildings on it were demolished. The Duke selected as architect for the new building George Gilbert Scott Junior, a convert to Catholicism. It would be dedicated to St. John the Baptist, in memory of the chapel in Maddermarket Street. The style was to be Early English Gothic. It would be immense. There seems to have been no competition, and the foundation stone was laid on the 17 July 1884.

Holy Apostles was closed in August 1894 upon the opening of the nave of the newly-built St. John the Baptist Catholic Church. This church, at the corner of St. Giles and Earlham Road in Norwich, was begun in 1884 and finished in 1910. It became the East Anglian Catholic Cathedral in 1976. The redundant Willow Lane Chapel was converted into Willow Lane Catholic School, which opened in 1896. The school closed in 1968.

When you look at the population figures for Norwich they show that what was the country's second city grew steadily from the end of the seventeenth century (29,000) rising to 40,000 by 1786 followed by a slight decline in the early 1800s. However, growth was not as rapid as in most of the more industrial areas of Britain at the end of the nineteenth century and early twentieth century.

By the beginning of the twentieth century Norwich was a sizeable (111,700) and growing city, though growth was significantly affected by both World Wars and the depression of the 1920s and 1930s – the population was 126,000 in 1931 but only 121,000 in 1951. Even so, significant suburban growth created an opportunity to create the Parish of St.George's.

The development of our Parish and churches
In 1896 St. George's Parish was raised and property was bought in Fishergate (with £500 from Earl of Orford and £900 from the Duke of Norfolk). The property was the old Boys' Hospital, parts of which dated back to the seventeenth century and endowed by Thomas Anguish in his will of 1617. The parish was officially designated as St. George's Church but known by nearly everyone as 'Fishergate'. The Altar and several of the furnishings from the old Maddermarket Chapel were used (the Stations of the Cross were later erected in St. Boniface Church at Hellesdon), and the pews for Fishergate were taken from the old Jesuit chapel in Willow Lane after the Jesuits left in 1881. It is believed that the main hall of the church was the boys' classroom and the buildings to the east, with the Dutch gables, were the boys' living and sleeping quarters.

The architect J.R. Benest designed our beloved St. George's R.C. Church at Fishergate. He also designed the ill-fated Drill Hall in Chapel Field and the lovely

The Maddermarket Altar (left) and the Fishergate Altar

thatched fountain on Mousehold Heath which, with a stone and flint base and four drinking fountains, stood as a landmark for over 80 years.

A comparison between the internal views of St. John's Maddermarket and St. George's Fishergate (above) show many similarities and so seems to support the view that many of the furnishings were transferred from one to the other when the old church closed.

St. George's was opposite the fine old church of St. Edmund Fishergate which was one of the smaller churches of the City. Its dedication to the king of East Anglia, martyred in 869, would indicate a foundation of late Anglo-Saxon date. The tower has a distinctive outline, and the size of the buttresses suggests it may have been intended to stand higher. The nave and chancel were built in 1463.

The early days of the Parish of St. George's.

In the beginning the parish was seen as part of St. John's but in 1897 Fr. Henry Long took charge and started the process of registering a new and separate parish with its own priest. Fr. Long was renowned for making parish visits on horseback. This extract from a letter from Fr. Long to the Bishop, dated 5 October 1902 carries an address of Colwyn House, St. Saviours, Norwich. It starts with the news that Fr. Long's mother had died ' after much suffering' and then goes on:

Having now been six years at St. George's I feel that a change of place & people very

St. Edmund's: our ancient neighbour in Fishergate

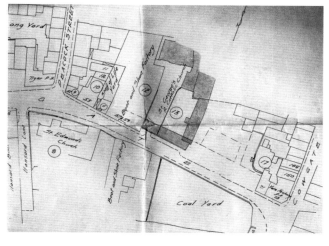

This 1930 plan by the City Engineers' Department shows the location of St. George's Fishergate and the neighbouring buildings – mainly industrial. The plan was drawn up at a time of road widening when a small piece of the land at the front of the church was sold to the City for £100

desirable, and should be glad if your Lordship would appoint me to another mission whenever you have a suitable vacancy. My tenancy at Colwyn House terminates at Xmas next.

I remain your obedient servant in JC. Fr. Long.

St. George's was formally recognised as a Parish in 1899 – that is, it became an ecclesiastical district. The Priest's residence was in Golden Dog Lane off Magdelan Street and the name first recorded in the *Liber Baptizatorum* (Register of Baptisms) was that of Catherine Weaver, born on the 22 October and baptised on the 5 November 1899. Her mother bore the surname of Rump; Catherine subsequently married on the 11 May 1920 in Ontario, Canada. In those early years of the parish it is interesting to see the large number of baptisms registered where the parents' address is given as one of the two military barracks nearby,

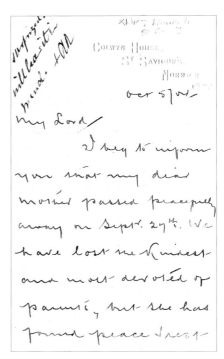

'I beg to inform you that may dear mother passed peacefully away': a letter to the Bishop from Fr. Long Fr. Long (1897-1906), dated 5 October 1902

names such as: Barnes, Bolden, Brock, Brundell, Carter, Clarke, Duncan, Forster, Harris, Henderson, Mullholland, Owen, Rudling, Russell, Walsh and Wray. This gives the first clear indication of a strong link between parish and barracks.

An examination of Confirmation lists from the turn of the nineteenth century shows 32 family names of 53 *confirmandii*: Ashurst, Batley, Barnham, Capstick, Cheyne, Clarke, Clickmore, Coe, Cottrell, Eaves, Gooch, Glasheen, Grehon, Grimes, Guigglestone, Hawes, Holmes, Jones, Liddimint, Middleton, Moore, Morris, Mountain, Mullholland, Muncey, Muskett, Newton, Rout, Russell, Shepherd, Starling and Wray. These provide a reasonable sampling of Catholic families practising in St. George's Parish in the early 1900s.

Interestingly the Confirmation names chosen were Joseph (x10), George (x4), Francis (x2) and then once each for Aloysius, Paul, Peter, Thomas, Benedict and John. For girls it was Maria (x13), Agnes (x5), Teresa (x5) Margarita (x3) and then once each for Cecilia, Anna, Winifred, Monica, Helena, Magdalena and Josephine.

The earliest recorded wedding in the parish was celebrated on the 5 May 1902, between Thomas Brogan and Elizabeth Forster with John and Susannah Brown as their witnesses.

An examination of the *Liber Defunctorum* (register of deaths) gives us some clues about social and health issues of a particular time. The five-year year period between 1900 and 1904 shows that of 36 deaths recorded in this parish, 19 (53%)

were of persons under 10 years of age, with an average age for all deaths of only 26 years. Compare those figures to 1964 when of 24 recorded deaths, only two (8%) were under ten, with an average age at death of 58.4 years. In 1990 only one of 33 deaths were under ten with an average age at death of 74.3 years.

Norwich at the time of the new St. George's Parish

A picture of Norwich at the time St. George's Parish started can be gleaned from an excellent study by J.J. McLean [4] which provides insights into Norwich as two cities, socially at least. One being the picturesque provincial centre, the other a city of slum living. The very poor living conditions, often based around over-crowded 'Yards' were prevalent in the area around and including Fishergate. Housing conditions in inner Norwich were horrendous for many.

> The unhealthy housing conditions were further exacerbated by the design and construction of the many 'Yards' in the City. This was a form of design and construction which had developed since the eighteenth century, and provided housing for a large number of residents. Each yard, usually in the form of a cul-de-sac, had a narrow entrance from a main thoroughfare leading to houses with a common yard. These yards, many of which were in poor areas, were poorly ventilated and badly lit, and had sanitary facilities which were primitive and communal. Being in close proximity to the Wensum, they posed serious health problems to the people who inhabited them, in addition to those hazards to which they were already exposed from their industrial neighbours.

> Yards contained a variable number of houses and inhabitants; in St. John's Head Yard off Coslany St.., there were reckoned at one time to be as many as 46 families! It was calculated that there were around 650 such Yards within the city environs, mostly around Oak St.., St. Benedict's, St. Martin's, Bottolph St.., Fishergate, Cowgate and Barrack St. Several bore intriguing and exotic names; Mulberry Yard and Seven Stars Yard, off St. Benedict's, and Eight Fingers Yard and White Bear Yard off Oak St.

McLean also reminds us that immigration was a key feature in the increase in population in and around the city and introduces us to a family which was to become very well known in the city and in the parish in particular:

> Immigrants also came from abroad to swell the numbers, bringing with them their skills, trades and endeavours. Among them in the early 1900s came seven Valori brothers from Tuscany, whose consortium soon specialised in making alabaster plaques and figurines from their premises in Ber St. and Bottolph St. In 1910 two of the brothers, Arturo and Armando opened, in Bishop Bridge Rd., the first of several fish and chips shops. In later years the family became firmly established and well- known in the city as also being purveyors of ice cream and cafe and restaurant owners.

The Valori family were well known in the Catholic community of St. George's. [5]

THE REST OF THE WORLD IN 1899

25 February: In an accident at Grove Hill, Harrow, Edwin Sewell became the world's first driver of a petrol-driven vehicle to be killed; his passenger, Maj. James Richer, died of injuries three days later.

9 March: Charles C. Wakefield began the lubricating oil company which became Castrol.

27 March: Guglielmo Marconi successfully transmitted a radio signal across the English Channel.

1 May: The National Trust acquired its first part of Wicken Fen, making it the UK's oldest wetland nature reserve.

17 May: Foundation stone of the Victoria and Albert Museum was laid by Queen Victoria, it was her last public engagement. At that time, in the 62nd year of her reign, she became Britain's longest-serving monarch.

19 June: Edward Elgar's Enigma Variations premiered in London.

6 September: The White Star Line's transatlantic ocean liner *RMS Oceanic* sailed on her maiden voyage. At 17,272 gross tons and 704 ft. (215 m), she was the largest ship afloat, following the scrapping of the *SS Great Eastern* a decade earlier.

11 October: Second Boer War began in South Africa.

15 November: The American Line's *SS St. Paul* became the first ocean liner to report her imminent arrival by wireless telegraphy when Marconi's station at The Needles contacted her 66 nautical miles off the coast of England.

8 December: The Aldeburgh life-boat capsized on service: seven of the eighteen crew were killed.

Also in 1899

The school-leaving age in England and Wales was raised to twelve.

Liquorice Allsorts were first marketed by Bassetts of Sheffield.

Oxo beef stock cubes were introduced by Liebig's Extract of Meat Company.

Bede was declared a Doctor of the Church by Pope Leo XIII, the only Englishman so named.

The Valori family, specialising in making alabaster plaques and figurines and later fish and chips!

1906 brought about the first of several changes in parish priest. Fr. Long moved to Ely and the new parish priest was Fr. Edward Scott. In this letter from Fr. Scott, again with the address Colwyn House, St. Saviour's, Norwich and dated 5 September 1907 illustrates the perennial problem of feeling out on a limb, particularly in a huge Diocese centred on Northampton, as well as illustrating that much of the written correspondence between the priests and the Bishop was to do with dispensations for mixed faith marriages – he says:

> My Lord,
> Thanks for reply to the dispensation for marriage. I was sorry to hear you had been so ill. We get little news here from other parts of the diocese, and I had not heard anything of your…illness …

On the Feast of the Immaculate Conception, 8 December 1910, the great church of St. John's was opened with a Blessing and Pontifical High Mass celebrated by the Bishop of Northampton, Dr. Keating. Within the lifetime of people who had known the end of the penal years, the greatest Catholic Church in England was complete.

In August 1912 the River Wensum (the southern boundary of the parish)

August 1912: the Wensum floods the city

flooded to a depth of 3 feet; the surrounding area and Fishergate fabric was extensively damaged. For over twelve hours on Monday, 26 August, East Anglia, and Norfolk in particular, was deluged by an almost tropical downpour – railway, telephone and road communications with the outside world being almost entirely cut off and immense damage to property ensuing, both in Norwich and the country districts. In twelve hours close to six inches of rain had fallen – an astonishing amount when just one inch brings 100 tons of water per acre.[6]

Also in August 1912 Norwich hosted the third National Catholic Congress chaired by the Cardinal Archbishop of Westminster. The *The Eastern Daily Press* published a remarkable welcome:

> The National Catholic Congress will bring many visitors to Norwich today, and, while many will agree to differ from them in opinion, Norwich citizens generally will welcome their visitors and hope that they will have the pleasantest of times in the old city.[7]

The Congress was also national news:

GREAT GATHERING AT NORWICH. A CIVIC WELCOME
The third National Catholic Congress initiated a new departure by meeting at a city and in a district with no large Catholic population. But it was foreseen by the Cardinal that these yearly gatherings could not and should not be restricted to great centres of population ; and for the new departure Norwich, as a city full of historic associations with the Catholic past, with a church of almost cathedral proportions and magnificence, and a population generally indifferent to Catholicism, offered at once many advantages for the meeting and a field for work. From London, at any rate, there was a goodly company of visitors. Many travelled down early, and many more left Liverpool

Street by the train which conveyed the Cardinal, the Archbishop of Birmingham, and the Duke of Norfolk at 1.35 p.m. Though the Great Eastern Railway Company accorded little consideration in the way of special accommodation, the journey down was less unpleasant than it might have been, thanks to a fresh breeze and a fleecy sky, which tempered the sun's heat. The country through which the train passed rolled away on either side of the line in swelling undulations of vivid green, lined with the darker green of the hedgerows and woods framing lighter patches of grain yellowing to ripeness. Arrived at Thorpe Station, Norwich, the travellers poured from the train upon the narrow platform, and the cheers that rose told us that the Cardinal had alighted, and was being welcomed with the enthusiasm which has always characterised such occasions.

For the full coverage of the congress, including an insight into how Catholics were viewed in Norwich just over 100 years ago and what issues were of concern to the Church, a visit to *The Tablet* online archive is a must.[8] The report provides a fascinating snapshot of contemporary views on religion: views that have a resonance today in attitudes to Judaism, Islam and the other great religions of the world.

A contrasting view is illustrated by this thoughtful letter from a Norwich citizen in the *Norwich Evening News*:

The general feeling of Norwich citizens is, I am convinced, one of friendly welcome to the visitors, and by consenting, with characteristic courtesy, to be present at the Friday evening meeting, the Lord Mayor has rightly interpreted the general spirit. It remains for imported extremists to endeavour to harrow our feelings by prominent posters, and to suggest that the Congress is a Papal attempt to capture Norwich. Of course, only the ill-informed fanatics will allow their sleep to be disturbed by the 'grim prospect.' It is regrettable, however, that a local clergyman should have taken a hand in the game. He must know, as I think any man of observation knows, that it is the growth of agnosticism that is the danger rather than the spread of Roman Catholicism or any other set of beliefs. For an example of broad-mindedness worthy of emulation let us turn to the many quiet acts of charity and kindness done by the Roman Catholic 'Little Sisters' to our slum dwellers, irrespective of the latter's creed. But perhaps we shall be asked to believe that this is another and more subtle attempt of the Pope to capture Norwich. The State itself sets an example to the individual by not defining the limits of toleration, and certainly the spiritual welfare of the people is advanced by charitable actions rather than by floods of uncharitable rhetoric in the Market Place.[9]

Life around the parish and in Norwich in the 1920s and 1930s
The parish population changed significantly with decline immediately around Fishergate and expansion from the new estates at Mile Cross, Sprowston and around the Plumstead Road area.

J.J. McLean's study provides a very readable analysis of housing policy after the First War and through the 1920s and 30s. He shows how gradually the slums

Fr.Scott 1906-1935. 'If you all gave Fr. Scott 1/2d each week he would have enough to live on'

of inner Norwich were removed and large scale public housing estates grew around Norwich especially in areas linked to the parish:

> The first tract of land to be purchased by compulsory order for demolition in August, 1931 was Sun Yard, in Coslany ward, comprising a multitude of houses and, in close proximity, 3 shoe factories, a silk and textile manufacturer, a brewery and an iron works. Between 1931 and 1935 extensive demolition also took place around Barrack St., and Little Bull Close, as well as relatively minor eradication of unfit housing and places of manufacture in Ber St.., Bottolph St. and Fishergate. Additional slum areas identified included Rising Sun Lane, Grout's Thoroughfare, Timberhill, Cat and Fiddle Yard and Distillery Yard with a population of 8000. Later phases would include Heigham St.., Derby St.., Colegate, Finkelgate, Rosary Rd., Pottergate and St. Giles St.

It was impossible to cope with such a massive programme of demolition and simultaneous reconstruction and rehousing on the same sites, and the council sought to extend the new estates or acquire additional land for housing. By 1930 new developments were planned or under way on Mousehold estate with provisional designation for 100 houses rising to 400, plus 100 at Catton, which would be later increased to 550 and land was also purchased at Larkman Lane. To help alleviate the wider problems of poverty and unemployment at this time, schemes were also introduced to provide employment for men out of work.[10]

Ian Brundell (parishioner and Eucharistic minister at Our Lady's Thorpe) remembered in 2012:

> Around 1923 or 1924 there was a church cycling club, I don't remember whether it was run by St. John's or St. George's, but young men and women from both parishes

Fr.Donald Hillier.

Fr. Hillier (*top*) and Fr. Pritchard

used to cycle out together, that's how my mum and dad met. The favourite ride was out to 'Little Switzerland' either on the North Walsham Road. [Little Switzerland is an old chalk excavation near Coltishall that was abandoned many years ago or it may have been Brundall Gardens, a leisure area of 120 acres known as The Switzerland of Norfolk.] It was a very good way of young people meeting together and enjoying the outdoors. [11]

About 30 years ago the parish history group started collecting reflections from its members. Looking back at the original Parish Church during Fr. Scott's time they said:

The Church was always spoken of affectionately as Fishergate, never as St. George's, one visiting priest asked who St. Fishergate was!

Nothing was ever new at Fishergate. The benches and vestments, the odd pictures, organ (a wheezer, hand pumped and erratic) were all hand-me-downs. The once upon a time fine vestments came from the old Costessey Hall Chapel and constantly needed stitching.

The Catholic soldiers at the barracks used to march to church on Sunday for the 10.15 Mass, usually with a band.

When the Salvation Army used to play in the streets on Sundays the leader would halt the band when it passed the Church so the congregation could hear what was going on.[12]

Catherine Middleton remembers being a pupil at Willow Lane between 1924 and 1933 and Sr. Madeline from Notre Dame getting all the children who went to Fishergate to stand up – 'if you all gave Fr. Scott 1/2d each week he would have enough to live on' – the parish was relatively poor and the parish Priest was poor too. Fr. Scott had moved from the house in Golden Dog Lane to a small cottage next to the church. Fr. Scott died there in 1935 at the age of 72.

Memories of life in the parish during the Second World War

From 1935 to 1941 there was no parish priest but the community was well served by Fr. Guy Pritchard and Fr. Donald Hillier from St. John's. The parish was expanding rapidly in size and the Development Fund was started to cater for future needs and expansion.

Fr. Pritchard was a Felixstowe man born in 1913 and serving many Parishes across East Anglia. He left Norwich to become Army Chaplain for six years and served in France and Burma. In peacetime he was officiating Chaplain to the army for 12 years and to the RAF for 15 years.

While the spiritual needs of the people of the parish were well served by its bigger brother and neighbouring parish of St. John's, the growth and feel of being a parish almost disappeared during these difficult years. Obviously St. John's had its own issues and priorities and growth in St. George's was left some way behind. Parish records were not really kept in any systematic way and, to put it bluntly, the parish was broke. However, a plot of land was purchased, largely through the efforts of Fr. Pritchard who raised £400. The church was kept clean and a caretaker's cottage prepared for occupancy.

Life in the parish and the impact of the Second World War is still rich in the memory of several members of the parish community. In 1941 it was with great joy and relief to the community Fr. Edward Watkis was appointed as the new parish priest.

Top: Mgr. Canon Freeland on his retirement with three of the St. John's Clergy who served St. George's between 1935 and 1941 from left to right: Fr. John Thompson, Fr. Donald Hillier, Fr. Laurence Nicholson

Above: Fr Watkis became parish priest in 1941

It was a difficult time, there was no money in the bank. Fr. Watkis was told to expect £4.10.0 in the collection each week but it quickly doubled – an early sign of the commitment and generosity of the parish. On 15 August the presbytery was moved to No 92 Constitution Hill and a bus service commissioned from Thorpe for the early mass each Sunday. In October the Children of Mary was separated from the St. John's Council and Stella Palmer became our first President.

On the 27 April 1942 the full horror of the Second World War came to the streets of Norwich. Air raids caused damage to the Presbytery and Fr. Watkis had to move into St. Johns. Three members of the Holland family in Paterson Road were killed in an air raid and a member of the Harbach family in Waterloo Road as well and many were evacuated.

St. John's windows were blown out and the school closed for two weeks. Mile Cross Tavern which was used for Sunday Mass was damaged and Mass had to be discontinued. Permission was given for Mass to be said on Sundays at the Norman School, Kirkpatrick Road from the first Sunday in June.

June 26 and 27 saw further air raids and Fishergate was in the midst of the devastation. Gough's factory, next to the church was fired by incendiary bombs and the fire spread to the cottage adjacent to the church where the caretakers, Mr. and Mrs. Reginald Moore lived. The sacristy caught fire but Mr. Moore retrieved the Tabernacle key and removed the Blessed Sacrament to safety. Firemen saved the church but the sacristy and its contents were destroyed.

As the parish book of the time says:

> The Church was saved. But what chaos. The roof of the corridor went. Church full of rubble, Rush around looking for place for Mass.

A young man named Mullarkey during one night climbed on the roof of Fishergate and heroically pulled off an incendiary bomb. With great energy Fr. Watkis managed to find sanctuary in the Mayfair Cinema in Magdalen Street. A great sense of community and hard work ensured essential repairs were made and saved the church as a functioning house of worship. Again the parish book captures Fr. Watkis' mood very well:

> The Bishop comes from St. John's on Sat. evening to find me 'black'. 'Where are the things for Mass?' Luckily I have the Mile Cross Bag at my house. So I say 3 Masses in the Cinema on a Show Card from the foyer laid on top of the seats – I go to St. John's at night to see my people confirmed – but too tired to stay.

A determined attack was made upon Norwich Cathedral, around which no less than 850 incendiaries were showered, but owing to the efforts of the firewatchers and to the fact that the whole of the inside roofing is a vault of brick and stone, the only damage suffered was to the roofs of the north and south transepts, where some of the lead was melted and the timbers burnt. Two or three old houses in The Close were gutted including the Audit Chamber and one of the Grammar

School buildings.

Some reflections by two parishioners bring it very much to life for us:

> One Sunday during Mass a loudhailer was heard 'Knock if you can hear us' is what we kept hearing. This happened during the War in about 1942. A bomb had decimated the building opposite and people were trapped in the rubble.[13]

> We were very fortunate – when we came out of our Bacon Road house shelter several houses had been destroyed and every window bar one was broken - the only one left unbroken was protecting my statue of Mary and that night the family stayed in the only room with a window...Protected by Our Lady![14]

Catherine Middleton's statue – still pride of place in her home 70 years later

Archaeologically, Norwich lost more in this than in any previous raid. Ecclesiastical buildings, in addition to the Sacristy at Fishergate included the church of St. Michael at Thorn in Ber Street and the church of St. Paul's, both of which were burned out. In addition St. Julian's Church in King Street had almost everything excepting its north wall and porch completely annihilated by a high explosive bomb. St. Mary's Plain Baptist Church, which was accidentally burned a few days after the beginning of the war and had since been restored, was again gutted, this time hopelessly so, and with its adjoining schoolrooms. The Trinity Presbyterian Church in Theatre Street and the Synagogue in Synagogue Street were also badly damaged.

In August 1942, the parish's first curate, Fr. Patrick Carey arrived and, after the Mile Cross Tavern was damaged, Mass was offered for the Mile Cross community at the Norman School.

In 1943 Mass was offered once a month in the Heartsease Public House, Plumstead Road. In November negotiations commenced for the purchase of the site on Sprowston Road.

On 16 January 1944 Parishioners were shocked by the death of Father George Fressanges, attached to St. John's Church, Norwich, who died in the Ilford train crash when the Norwich to Liverpool Street train ran into the back of another train which had stopped at Ilford. In September that year Fr. Watkis was able to move into the presbytery at 221 Sprowston Road.

The parish history group gathered these memories some years ago:

During the war when the Italian and German POWs were in camps on Mousehold and at Brundell, Fr Watkis would go to say Mass for them. The Italian camps were very artistic with Madonnas painted everywhere and an air of grubbiness and joy everywhere. The German Camps were well organised and spick and span, spit and polish. When the war situation became easier the POWs were occasionally allowed to parade down to Fishergate on Sunday afternoon for a service. We English, with short memories, collected enough cigarettes for the men to have one each. The singing was wonderful. On one occasion the organist of Cologne Cathedral played the organ.

During the war, when as usual coke from the gas works came in barges up the river (2/- a sack if collected!) Fishergate had a real bonus. The shoe factory opposite had a good supply of coke in the yard when it was hit. The coke went up in the air, and crossed the road and landed in the Church drive and garden. Fr. Pritchard and Fr. Watkis were allowed to keep it and used it to heat the ancient clubroom where we had Sunday Mass.[15]

There were 18 USAAF airfields in Norfolk during World War Two, occupied by Bomb Groups flying B-17 Flying Fortresses and B-24 Liberator aircraft, and Fighter Groups providing support with their P-47 Thunderbolts, P-38 Lightnings and P-51 Mustangs. Traces of many airfields still exist today, and some are still operational (Horsham St. Faith is now home to Norwich International Airport and Hethel is the home of Lotus Cars).

The parish records[16] provide a fascinating insight into change in the parish at the end of the Second World War. In April, may, June and July of 1945 there were several weddings between local women and US servicemen, family names were:

Ayres / Kelly from New York City
Winter / Morgitan of Phoenixville Pennsylvannia
Bush / O'Keefe from St.Louis Missouri
Andrews / Chisum from Eagle Pass Texas
Stone / Klein from Dayton Ohio
Scales / Kohat from Rankin California
Shalders / Archaki from Cleveland Ohio
Bowles / Aldecoq from Little Rock, Arkansas.
Dwyer / Alden from Ronbury, Massachusetts.
Harvey / MIlewsky from Paterson, New Jersey.
Blowers / Langham from Mayfield, Kentucky.
Woodward / Dobies from Buffalo, New York.
Howard / Kent from Bell Island, Newfoundland.
Watering / Fiorillo from New York

Parish records showing the marriage of Francis Kohat USAAF of Rankin, California to Audrey Scales, 19 May 1945

Parish records showing the marriage of Vit Lubkiewicz, Polish Airforce at Coltishall, to Ruth Crowe, 20 September 1946

By March 1946 the RAF had the disbandment plans in hand. All Polish Air Force fighter squadrons were to relocate to Norfolk for disbandment. RAF Coltishall became the final home for No. 306, 309, 315 while 303 and 316 flew to Hethel. By April all transport squadrons based at Chedburgh (No. 301 and 304) ceased operations and the No. 318 Fighter-Reconnaissance Squadron was grounded in Italy before transferring to RAF Coltishall. The pilots, aircrew and ground crew were in turmoil and agony as they awaited the final order to disband with the role-out orders given over November 1946. Each Squadron marked the occasion with fly-past and marches to bands.

Between the end of 1944 and early 1947 there were several weddings involving service men from RAF Coltishall and RAF Horsham and mainly from the Polish Air Force stationed there. Families such as:

Holland / Strzatkowski;
Edmonds / Struk;
Crowe / Lubkiewicz;

The Altar and the Lady Altar in Fishergate

Kortkiewicz / Buchowiecki;
Warren / Jacknik
Lambert / Novak

On 10 June 1945 the *Parish Diary* said:

We held our usual procession of the Blessed sacrament, Benediction outside. Fr. Shar-bergh, American priest and Chaplain at USAF Rackheath carried the Monstrance. The Americans are leaving the neighbourhood, this made things quiet and the church less crowded.

And on 17 June we find some interesting short sentences perhaps illustrating the pressure an Episcopal Visitation provided:

First Episcopal visitation. All well. Font to be made to lock. He grants 'a privileged Altar'. A cheque for £1,000 is given to him for the Parish Extension Fund. He stays with us until Monday. Confirms on Monday evening. There were 53 candidates. Many convert wives of Americans. Church packed. Fr. Sharbergh assists by saying Mile Cross Mass. Fr. Flood, on a visit here assists for two Sundays. On third Sunday he says Mass at Brundell for Italian prisoners. They are now without Mass owing to Fr. Sharbergh's departure.[17]

Fr. Watkis with a First Communion group

At last, in January 1946, planning consent was granted for a new St. George's and in July Fr. Watkis turned his attention to a site in Thorpe St. Andrew. At this time The Children of Mary started as one of the parochial societies.

In January 1947 negotiations for the St. William's Way site began. Unfortunately, in the autumn Fr. Watkis resigned feeling that with the complex site negotiations a new priest with better health should take up the baton.

The Universal Church has been a key feature of our Catholic upbringing. The fact that Catholic worship, similar in nature can be found in all nations and cultures. Sometimes we think it is only a feature of recent twenty-first-century migration but this notice from the local newspaper provides a wonderful reminder of our links over many years and close links with the Polish community. It says:

POLISH CATHOLIC MEN AND WOMEN YOUR EASTER DUTIES
FATHER F TOMCZAK
Will hear Confessions in Polish at St. George's Catholic Church, Fishergate, Norwich, on Saturday, March 13th, at 7p.m., and Sunday March 14th, at 9.20 a.m. Nearest Bus Stops STUMP CROSS or Tombland. [18]

March 1947:
'FATHER F
TOMCZAK
Will hear Confes-
sions in Polish at
St. George's
Catholic Church'

**POLACY KATOLICY
WASZ OBOWIAZEK WIELKANOCNY**

Ks. Fr TOMCZAK
bedzie sluchal spowiedzi w jezyku
polskim w Kosciele Katolickim sw.
Jerzego na Fishergate w Norwich.

**Sobota, dn. 13 marca o godz. 19-tej
Niedziela, dn. 14 marca o g. 9.20 r.**

Najblizsze przystanki autobusowe
STUMP CROSS lub Tombland.

In 1948 was a year when Fr. Kevin Jones took on all the challenges. The Diocesan solicitors were instructed to effect the final purchase of the Sprowston Road site and at that time it became the property of the Church. Negotiations continued for the St. William's Way site on an expanded area.

Fr. Kevin Jones

CHAPTER 4

A Time of Expansion

The development of our three Churches: St. Georges Sprowston,

Our Lady's Thorpe and St. Boniface Hellesdon, 1949 to 1973

In January 1949 Fr. Jones was informed that an Air Ministry gymnasium and chapel in Brabazon Road, Hellesdon had been declared surplus to requirements and was available. Application was made to use the premises for religious purposes and planning consent was given in March; the site was purchased on a 25-year lease for £2,000.

A family man and a parishioner of St. George's, Bernard Williams, identified an opportunity to assist the spiritual development of his fellow male parishioners and at the same time use their talents in charitable work to provide help and support for those of his fellow parishioners, and others, who were less fortunate than himself. In considering how best to pursue this aim he came to the conclusion that this could best be achieved, in a structured and effective way, through the creation within the parish of a 'conference' of the St. Vincent de Paul Society (S.V.P.). Having received the active encouragement of the parish priest, Father Kevin Jones, Bernard contacted the S. V. P. National Office in London for help and guidance. In February the S.V.P. Conference was formed and aggregated to Supreme Council on 29 June. The president was Mr Bernard Williams and Secretary was Mr B Hardy.

You can get a glimpse of 'Fishergate' through this wonderful on-line recording in the University of East Anglia film archive, and get a real flavor of a post-war wedding. A professionally-produced record of the wedding of Mr Henry Woods and Miss Remina Valori describes how:

> On a cold and blustery November afternoon in 1949, guests arrive at the Roman Catholic Chapel of St. George in Fishergate, Norwich, to attend the wedding of Mr. Henry Woods and Miss Remina Valori. Departing from a property on the corner of Philadelphia Lane and Catton Grove North, the bridal party arrive at the chapel in a pair of Rolls Royce cars, followed by the bride, dressed in traditional white. Brief glimpses of the inside of the chapel show the ceremony underway, before the newly-weds emerge smiling and posing for photographs. The bridal party depart in the Rolls Royce cars with the guests following in a pair of coaches, all headed for the reception venue, the White Horse in Brundall. [1]

This following extract from the *East Anglian Guild Magazine* gives a good flavour of parish activity at that time:

In February, Miss R. Halligan gave us a clear, informative talk on the Schools' Question,

The parish church of St. George's Fishergate, commonly called 'Fishergate'. The building was adapted from the old Boys' Hospital buildings, parts of which were seventeenth century. The picture on right shows the Dutch porch

and a fortnight later four bus loads of us journeyed to Yarmouth to take part in the Schools' Rally at Britannia Pier, where Alderman Burn and Fr. John Murray, S.J., addressed a large gathering of East Anglian Catholics and non- Catholics.

To prepare us in part for Holy Year, Miss Gunton, of Cromer, kindly gave us an interesting, illustrated lecture on Rome.

The Brothers of St. Vincent de Paul are doing excellent work in the parish, in the homes and in the Prison, under the guidance of their spiritual director Fr. Kevin Jones. They deserve all our support and we are proud of them. Gifts of rosaries, prayer books,

clothes and footwear, together with our prayers, would help them in their work.

The blitzed sacristy is being rebuilt and in due course will need new furnishings.

We hope that all will interest themselves in the collections and in the social functions, which are being held to raise funds to increase the Parish Extension Fund. Much has to be done to prepare the Brabazon Road Gymnasium for a Mass Centre.

Spiritual facilities, social evenings and outings are arranged for the benefit of Italian, Irish and Polish girls in our parish. Fr. Bonomo spent another busy, pleasant week-end here. Fr. Stasz visited the parish last week-end.[2]

The following delightful story tells of the romance between a parishioner, Miss Patricia Williams and Mr. Giovanni Siano who met at St. George's, Fishergate. Mr. Siano attended the Church when he was a prisoner of war. They were refused permission to marry at first when Giovanni was repatriated but he was eventually offered a job on a farm at Great Plumstead and was granted a work permit after a tenacious campaign by Patricia through letters to British and Italian government departments and through the *Eastern Daily Press*. I met Patricia last year by chance at a display at Duxford and we talked about this story and she confirmed the whole thing as accurate and full of love.

Finally on 25 July 1950, the Church of St. Boniface, Hellesdon was solemnly opened and blessed by the Bishop, the Sacristy at Fishergate was rebuilt after its War damage and in December the St. William's Way site was finally purchased for £1,250. On the 14 December the Guild of St. Stephen for Altar Servers was inaugurated.

Norfolk Pow romance

The above photograph, taken at St. George's. Fishergate, Norwich, today, completes a chapter in a romance which began over three years ago, when the bride and bridegroom first met after attending a service in a Roman Catholic church.

The bridegroom, Mr. Giovanni Siano, was then an Italian prisoner of war in a camp near Norwich. He became engaged to his 20-year-old bride, Miss Patricia Agnes Josephine Williams, of 109, Mousehold Avenue, Norwich, before he was repatriated in May, 1946. but was refused permission to marry.

Then Miss Williams began writing. She wrote to the Italian Consul, the British Consul, the Ministry of Labour and National Service. She cannot remember how many letters she did write, but says it was "dozens and dozens."

In the end the Foreign Labour Division said Giovanni would be granted a permit to return if he had a job to come to.

Offered a Job

So Miss Williams wrote another letter. This time it was an appeal to the readers of the "Eastern Daily Press," and it was answered by Mr. G. B. Burtt, of Great Plumstead, who offered Giovanni a job on his farm.

In the meantime Miss Williams had faced another difficulty concerning her home. Her father died in 1945, and she lost her mother in May, 1946, and she did not want to give up the home where she and her husband will live. But after a few months' negotiating she was granted the tenancy.

Last summer Miss Williams went to Italy for her holiday, and visited her husband's family at Bracigliano, ten miles from Salerno, and saw her husband's vineyards.

Patricia couldn't remember how many letters she wrote but says it was 'dozens and dozens'

THE new Roman Catholic church of St. Boniface, Brabazon Road, Hellesdon, was blessed and opened by the Bishop of Northampton (Mgr. Leo Parker) yesterday when he offered the first Mass before a congregation of about 200.

The building, substantially constructed of concrete, was designed as a gymnasium for the St. Faiths airfield, but owing, it is stated, to an error, it was mistakenly sited in Brabazon Road and after the war was discarded as being too far from the station. The interior has been colour washed in cream with a light grey-blue roof. Altar rails and pulpit have been constructed of red brick and the altar is also supported on brick piers.

The new church replaces the former Sunday Mass centre at Norman School, Mile Cross, and is served from St. George's, Fishergate. The parish priest, Father Kevin Jones, said the building had been bought by means of St. George's development fund. The parish embraces all Norwich north of the river and another site for a church has been acquired on Sprowston Road near the Lazar House.

APOSTOLIC ZEAL

The Bishop explained that the church could not be consecrated as it was technically only a temporary building but he was very glad to come and say a few words of congratulation and joy that a new altar had been erected on which the sacrifice of Christ would be offered. For many years they had been very overcrowded at Fishergate and much of the population had moved outwards from the middle of the city.

Referring to the dedication of the church, Bishop Parker said St. Boniface was an Englishman imbued with great Apostolic zeal who went and evangelised Eastern Europe. Today they had need of his spirit, for it was from there that militant atheism was coming. England today had a great say in the future of Germany and it was a sad thing that our English politicians did not recognise the power of the Church in Germany.

Most of the congregation had to stand during the Bishop's address as the furnishing of the interior is not yet complete.

The picture shows Mgr. Leo Parker being received at the main entrance to the new church by the parish priest, Fr. Kevin Jones.

Eastern Daily Press 25 July 1950 reports the opening of The Church of St. Boniface, Hellesdon

The Italian influence and parish life in the 1950s and 60s

Fr. Jones was well known for his help for foreign workers, particularly Italian and Spanish around the early 1950s. The *Diocesan Magazine* in Spring 1951 shows how strong the Italian link was:

> many of the Italian girls whom we had grown to know and to like left us before Christmas (1950) to return to Italy. The linen altar cloth in use this Easter was made and given by them. Others have come to live and work among us and have found the Social Club a boon to them.[3]

The report goes on to describe visits to London to see the Italian Prime Minister, Italian classes given by Miss Anna Valori, and the parish dramatic society.

In addition to the strong Polish and Italian links the Catholic Community was enriched by migrants after the war from several countries that supported the British war effort and whose service men and women stayed in England or, because of home circumstances, had no chioce but to stay. Some of these new

Fr. Jones was well known for his help for foreign workers, particularly Italian and Spanish in the early 1950s. Here he arranged an excursion for women from F.W. Harmer & Co to the Italian Embassy. 'The girls' fares were paid by the factory management'

members of the community came from The Ukraine and other countries then being absorbed by the expanding Soviet Union.

At the same time there was great pride in being *English* Catholics, as this extract from the *Catholic Herald* shows:

> In view of recent correspondence in your paper on the subject of a suitable badge for English Catholics, you may possibly be interested in our own. Consisting of Saint Peter's Keys on Saint George's Cross, it proclaims not only our membership of St. George's Church but also our allegiance to Saint Peter's See. At the same time it honours Saint George as England's Protector and Saint Peter as our Patron Saint. P. W. Diem, Secretary, The Association of Saint George, St. George's Church. Fishergate, Norwich.[4]

Interviewers with parishioners paint an evocative picture of the parish as it came to grips with post-war austerity:

> The décor at Fishergate – pews were painted very dark brown. There was a metal grate at the church entrance and it always clanged when people stood on it. Quite a lot of people were late for Mass, the grate was a give away!

> There was a dear old gentleman at the church called Mr. Mullarky who had long grey locks down to his shoulders. Once a soldier offered Mr. Mullarkey some money but he said, 'keep it son – you need it more than me.'[5]

With Fr. Jones at the Italian Embassy

The Valori family, hard-working immigrants from Tuscany whose single-mindedness and hard work built businesses and influence in the city: front row – Mum (Rosa or Rosina neé Mancini), Remina, Giovanni, Peirina, Eva and Dad (Guido); back row: Remo, Guido, Francesco, Orlando, Gino and Reggie

Parish life in the 1950s:
a Fitzmaurice
family christening

A First Holy Communion group in the 1960s with Fr Roberts

The parish Youth Club was started and became well known for its Apostolic zeal. Classes in foreign languages were given to aid the integration of overseas workers. Melinda Warrington remembers:

> Fr. Kevin Jones started the Sunday night youth club to encourage the Italian girls to meet more nationalities. Harmers (the clothing factory) had recruited the girls to work for them. … and the effort put into getting to Mass – My mum took my sister and me to Fishergate every Sunday. We walked up Gordon Avenue, through the Plumstead Road Estate, down Gas Hill, along Bishopgate, around a high wall and eventually we got to Fishergate exhausted. I was 7 years old and my sister 3 years, I think she must have been in a pushchair, but I can't remember.[6]

Veronica Short's Brownie Pack: 'I remember playing Dodge Ball in the courtyard'

In a lovely little piece in the *Eastern Daily Press* in the early 1960s Geoffrey Goreham wrote a piece in a series about Norwich heritage as follows about St. George's Chapel:

> Overlooked by factory buildings and the silent church of St., Edmund, St. George's Chapel, in Fishergate, lies tucked away beyond an old wall and a patchy forecourt. It is a small, serene building, rich in flint and ornate brickwork with large church-like windows reaching to a low, sloping grey-slate roof, where tiny dormer windows look out across the yard.
>
> To a visitor finding the chapel for the first time it is something of a surprise. Like most buildings of its kind, it has an amiable eccentricity, the result of practical rebuilding clashing with a desire for style. A chapel of ease to St. John the Baptist Church, this little Catholic mission adds interest to an area dominated by warehouses and box factories and where even the medieval church of St. Edmund is a store for merchandise.[7]

Another parishioner, Veronica Short remembered an early childhood at Brownies in Fishergate in the early 1960s:

> I remember playing Dodge Ball in the courtyard which involved dodging a ball as it was thrown forcefully at your legs ....the aim of the thrower was to hit you below the knee and the aim of the player was to dodge the ball .. which you did your best to do as it did really hurt if you got hit ! I also remember that the loo was down a very dark scary passage which ran, as I remember, down the side of the church to the left as you looked

A Parish group from the 1950s with Fr. Kevin Jones

Veronica Short's family – a summer wedding at St. George's Fishergate

at the building from the road. The loo was outside and there were no lights at all.
I remember being surrounded by large families (the Crooks, Williams, Alcocks, Larters, Beasleys, Valori, Fitzmaurices, Molloys) that I went to school with to Willow Lane and to church. It was a happy secure time and despite the outside loos and (in hind sight) poor facilities I was happy. Later my parents moved to the other side of the city and I really missed being part of this vibrant and happy community.

Parish life in the 1970s

We have now reached the 1970s in our story. What was Parish life like at that time? Fr. Bosco Clarke, who retired from Marlow in 2010 remembered his early days at St. George's, his first parish. He was here from 1968 to 1971 and records 'I will always be grateful for the welcome I received from Fr. Tony Roberts and Fr. John Smith but above all from the people of the parish. It has always been the wonderful people of parishes I served in that sustained me in my ministry.'

Between April and June 1970 the altar was repositioned to its current place – moving a wonderful piece weighing some 2 tons was carried out by Carters and George Scarlett Ltd.

In 1971 the church was actively involved in two national radio broadcasts including the *Sunday Half-Hour* and later Bishop Clark's broadcast on the World Service.

In the early 1970s the development of the new building at St. William's Way, Thorpe St. Andrew was announced, to comprise a church and junior school. Gaining approval for the new building was not easy: plans were turned down because the council (then Blofield and Flegg R.D.C) considered the building would not be of adequate quality; there was also concern about noise and that the car park would give an untidy appearance from St. William's Way. Modifications were made and the plans approved subject to some landscaping changes.

So it was that the Church of Our Lady, Mother of God was established on St. William's Way. The building was a simple, straightforward construction seating about 200 and costing £17,000 plus a further £2,000 for furnishings; the car park, access road and landscaping cost a further £7,000. In February 1972 the new chapel was blessed by the Right Rev. Alan Clark. Assisting the Bishop with the ceremonies were Fr. Anthony Roberts, Francis Hanley, Mark Allcock, Mark Keelan, Paul Larter and Andrew Mynett.

The parish newsletters took on a familiar shape and each week tried to keep the parish informed and encouraged, a study of the newsletters shows that a number of themes emerged which say much about the parish and its focus. The themes included: peace; education; prayer; support for victims of catastrophes; collections and good deeds; the missions; pilgrimage; clubs and activities. These provide a useful reminder as to the priorities of a Catholic parish.

Mrs Newman Sanders, wife of a local television presenter, and known as Maggie throughout the parish, wished to enhance the social life of the parish by arranging regular lunch meetings with other parishioners. These were to be held

Scouts ready for parade and 'trendy' young parishioners, both around 1970

Fr. Clarke with some children at their First Communion (c.1970)

in Maggie's own home in Old Catton, and so began the St. George's Luncheon Club. Meetings took place on the second and fourth Wednesdays of the month and after a cooked meal the ladies, (no gentlemen at this time), capitalised on the opportunity to have a fulfilling chat.

In the early 1970s there was a wonderful celebration in the church: a concelebration of thanksgiving for 25 years in the priesthood for Mgr. Alan Clark (then Bishop of Elmham) and Fr. Anthony Roberts. The church was decorated with arum lilies, lilac, copper beech leaves, carnations and many other flowers. It was attended by some 100 clergy and nuns from the diocese and beyond. Besides the Bishop of Northampton, The Rt. Rev. Charles Grant the congregation included brothers of the two concelebrants, Mgr. Paul Clark from Weybridge and Fr. Christopher Roberts from Northampton.

Eastern Daily Press, 8 February 1972

NEW R.C. CHAPEL AT
−8. FEB. 1972
THORPE BLESSED

Churches

AFTER many years of hearing Mass in a schoolroom with an improvised altar Roman Catholics at Thorpe now have a chapel of their own at St. William's Way.

On Sunday morning the Bishop of Elmham, the Right Rev. Alan Clark, blessed the chapel and announced that it would be known as Our Lady, Mother of God. He said "Very few churches are dedicated this way, but it is her greatest title," and described the building as simple, straightforward

The building, which seats about 200, cost just under £17,000, furnishings were a further £2000 and site works — including car park, access road and landscaping which were insisted upon by the planners — £7000 more.

Assisting the Bishop with the ceremonies were the parish priest, Father Anthony Roberts, Mr. Francis Hanley, Mark Allcock, Mark Keelan, Paul Larter and Andrew Mynett.

Following the Mass the congregation joined the Bishop for refreshments at a nearby

The Church of Our Lady, Mother of God was established next to St. William's Way, Thorpe St. Andrew

Fr. Roberts' Jubilee. He departed in April 1974

During this time the parish church was active in the media, for example on 12 October 1973, BBC Radio 2 presented *Sunday Half-Hour*:

from St. George's Church, Norwich. Introduced by Fr. John Thompson: Prayer and Blessing, and conductor of combined choirs, Fr. Anthony Roberts; organist, Geoffrey Laycock. [8]

In 1974 Fr. Roberts left in April and a new parish priest, Fr. Robert Manley was appointed.

CHAPTER 5

Recent times

Some key events from the end of the twentieth century

The *Parish Report* for 1974 helps us look into the parish of that time. The parish clergy were: Fr. Robert Manley, Fr. Anthony Foreman and Fr. Roy Gathercole. Mr. Geoffery Laycock (choirmaster and organist) reluctantly stepped down after great service which saw music in the parish grow from strength to strength. The estimated Catholic population was about 3,000, with 1,185 mass attendances and 62 baptisms and 35 weddings that year. The main organisations listed were the SVP; Ladies Guild; Guild of St.Stephen; Third World Group; 21st. Norwich Guides (with 25-30 children per meeting); the Scout Group (25 scouts); Lunch Club; Catton Family Group and the Senior Club.

The Luncheon Club grew significantly in 1974. The parish priest Fr. Manley, readily agreed to the use of the St. George's Parish Hall. This new venue with its enlarged and more suitable facilities soon enabled the creation of other 'fun' activities which, in turn, brought about more new members. These 'after lunch' activities encouraged the indulgence of a 'flutter' through such pastimes as bingo and whist. At this time membership ranged from 30 to 40 regular diners paying as much as 20p per meal in these early days. The sister club, Hellesdon Lunch Club ran concurrently with St. George's and provided lunches each month right up to the time it closed in 1986. Entertainment after lunch was organised on a very similar basis as at St. George's.

Maggie Newman-Sanders with her usual enthusiasm and energy initiated the organisation of coach trips to relatively local venues. Their early popularity very soon resulted in trips being arranged each month and involved local places of interest such as zoos, public gardens, seaside resorts etc.

Rev. Anthony Foreman (curate at St. George's 1974-1976) wrote to remind me of the famous cartoons produced by Paul Jarvis which became such a feature of Parish Life in the 1970's. Fr. Foreman came to St. George's as curate in 1974 succeeding Fr. Frank McDerrmot and left in 1976. He left to take on his first parish at Sudbury.

On 13 March 1976, by the decree *Quod Ecumenicum*, Pope Paul VI caused the Diocese of Northampton to be split in two, and the three eastern counties of Cambridgeshire, Norfolk and Suffolk formed the new Diocese of East Anglia. Bishop Alan Clark (1919-2002) became the First Bishop of East Anglia. From mid-way through the year those receiving Holy Communion were able to receive the Host in their hand as a part of receiving the Sacrament.

Mike Howlings, a highly respected member of the parish community for many years provided a clear account of parish life in the last quarter of the twentieth century:

This Christmas cartoon depicts
Anthony Foreman (left),
Fr. Bob Manley (centre) and
Roy Gathercole (right)

In 1975/6 one of the members of the SVP, a farm owner working a farm just north of Norwich, kindly donated an on going supply of pre-packed bags of potatoes for needy families and this continued for some two years which made a welcome and helpful supplement to the normal provisions distributed.

St. George's became twinned with a conference in Grenada. The main support provided was the transfer of cash direct to the twinned conference and the sending of second hand tools, donated by parishioners, to encourage individuals into employment, however small. Grenada is still the recipient of the aid forwarded from St. George's.

Each year on the first Sunday of July, East Anglian Central Council organise, on behalf of the National Council, a pilgrimage for the sick to Our Lady's National Shrine at Walsingham. The highlight of the day is an open air Mass at 13.30 celebrated normally by the Bishop of East Anglia, during which each of the sick is anointed. This day is one that is fondly anticipated by all as it provides a very welcome opportunity for members, from all over the UK, to meet and share experiences with their fellow Vincentians.[1]

The *Parish Report* of 1977 shows some of the changing life of the parish following Vatican II. The parish clergy were Fr. Robert Manley, Fr. Roy Gathercole, Fr. Bede Edwards O.D.C. joined by Rev. Thomas Newland as Deacon. After Vatican II we saw the welcome introduction of extra-ordinary Eucharistic Ministers with the first four in our parish, Francis Hanley, Raymond Howlings, Paul Jarvis and Thomas Newland, commissioned by the Bishop in January. The estimated

Fr. Manley with a Parish group on the lawn, with Judy Reynolds on the right next to Fr. Gathercole and Fr. Foreman. In the centre is Ray Howlings and front left is Ben the dog

Fr. Manley (left) with fellow clergy in the late1970s

Catholic population of the parish was about 3,500 with 1,270 mass attendances on average 56 baptisms and 27 weddings.

New organisations and clubs appeared: Keep Fit for the over 60's; the Brabazon Wine Club; and a growing ecumenical movement around Sprowston Community Welfare. The parish was very large – trying to service five churches including continuing with Fishergate and St. Helen's at Hoveton as well as serving four hospitals and the prison. The size of the Christmas offering that year gives an indication of the relative size of the congregations in each church; 68% at St. George's; 13% at Hoveton; 7% each at St. Williams and Hellesdon and 5% still at Fishergate.

In some of the early newsletters during this year the parish priest appealed for the lay readers to read with greater clarity and meaning. This showed some of the tension around when changes in the liturgy, which we now take for granted, were relatively new to the priests and the parish community.

Mr. Thomas Newland who was ordained
as one of our first deacons

In 1977 Norwich was chosen to be the host venue for the National A.G.M. of the St. Vincent de Paul Society. Two brothers from St. George's Conference undertook the main work necessary to provide for all the delegates over the weekend of the 16 to 19 September. All the accommodation, together with meals, and the lecture theatres required for discussion sessions, were provided at the University of East Anglia. The main meeting on Sunday 18 September took place in St. John's Cathedral under the chairmanship of the Rt. Rev. Alan Clark, Bishop of East Anglia, followed by Mass of the Day.

The other huge development for the parish was when Notre Dame School opened its doors in September as a new, Co-Ed and fully Comprehensive Voluntary Aided School, with 850 students of which 72 were boys. Sister Mary S.N.D. was the first principal, Joanne Lovelock the first head-girl and Jane Beardshaw first deputy head-girl.

The *Eastern Daily Press* on 17 December 1977 carried a heart-warming article about Mr. Thomas Newland who was ordained as one of our first deacons. Thomas lived in Catton and had been very active in the wider community supporting youth and community work in Sprowston, a district councillor and school governor. The story went on to describe how Mr Newland officiated at the first wedding at St. Boniface Church. The wedding was for Mr. Frank Stannard (72) and Mrs. Vera Pope (66). Tom Newland had been Frank's best man at his first wedding some 45 years previously. Frank had been the sacristan at St. Boniface from the early 1950s but the church was only licensed for weddings in 1977. The couple had met at the luncheon club!

Mike Howlings reflected on the early developments of music in St. George's:

From the time when we started to celebrate the Church's liturgy in the new and beautiful church of St. George, the choir went from strength to strength and was recognised by the media in the broadcasting of sung services both on radio and on television. The choir was now singing, with success, the polyphonic setting of the Common of the Mass by Victoria and Palestrina, one of the future hopes of Fr. Roberts set out in 1959. The choir was most fortunate to count amongst its members real local professional talent. Two requiring special mention: Joan Rowe a well known Norwich pianist and a keyboard tutor who had also served the local community as an assistant Choirmaster for the Norwich Philharmonic Choir. Joan undertook to be an assistant organist when Geoffrey was directing the choir. One interesting anecdote concerning Joan related to her physical stature, being rather petite. The problem she encountered when playing the organ was her inability to adequately reach the foot pedals and on one occasion when playing at a parish wedding she had to ask one of her piano students to play these very necessary pedals so as to satisfy the request from the married couple for the playing of Widor's Organ Symphony No. 6, during the wedding ceremony. The other person requiring special mention was Vivian Morris, a music teacher at Notre Dame High School who, not only was he proficient in reading music but he possessed a true Welsh tenor voice which the parishioners enjoyed on the major feast days of the year.[2]

Fr. Roy Gathercole left to become Parish Priest at Poringland and Fr. Selman left to become Chaplain at Cambridge University. The clergy taking the parish into the 1980s were Fr. Robert Manley, Fr. Peter Leeming, Fr. Richard Healey and Rev. Thomas Newland as Deacon. The estimated Catholic Population at the time was about 3,250 with 1,077 mass attendances on average.

The new parish Hall at Thorpe St. Andrew was opened but it was with great sadness the Church at Fishergate had to close temporarily in 1981, unfortunately the fabric of the building became dangerous and too expensive to maintain. The church was finally closed at the end of 1982 and the site is now part of Smurfit Kappa Norboard making a range of products: display boards, boards for the retail industry and specialist liners.

The popular Luncheon Club brought about a more stable membership, including some men and provided a popular social aspect of parish life. Coach trips continued in the summer months and were still enthusiastically supported.

Fr. Manley's long struggle with illness meant that reluctantly he had to give up his role as parish priest in the second half of 1982 and Fr. Leeming went to take up a role at Cambridge. The parish was lucky to get a new parish priest, Fr. Tony Rogers. Supported by Fr. Richard Healey; Fr. Simon Talbott and Decon Rev. Thomas Newland. This was also the year of the visit of Pope John Paul to Britain. As today world events had an impact on the parish and also helps us gain a clear picture of those early days in the 1980s. Mike Howlings says:

During this period the UK experienced an influx of people from the far east, particularly from Vietnam. Whilst accommodation was found by Norwich City and other Councils, charitable organisations were asked to assist where possible in the provision of furniture, bedding and clothing etc. As a number of these migrants were Catholics,

'Part of our Catholic history has gone' said Fr. Manley. St. George's Fishergate closed at the end of 1982, five months after this article appeared suggesting the buidling would be demolished

the SVP members were pleased to assist wherever they could. The Parish enjoy, to this day, the presence and friendship of these residents in our midst.[3]

Fr. Robert Manley died on the 8 February 1983, aged just 62. The parish produced a wonderful little book *A Motley Miscellany* reproducing a number of his famous and often humorous articles from 1970 to 1982. He was a regular contributor for many years to the 'Christian Viewpoint' column in the *East Anglia Daily Times,* and was Anglia TV's religious adviser on Catholic affairs. His Requiem Mass took place on 14 February at St. George's attended by some 60 colleague priests. Tony Rogers – parish priest from 1983 to 1989 reflected on this very difficult time for the parish and his welcome to his new role:

Following the death of Fr. Bob Manley, I arrived at St. George's in April 1983. When the presbytery was built in the 1960s, it was quite something, built on a scale that was not common at the time. At Fr. Bob's funeral there were lots of comments among the clergy about measuring up the curtains, but it came as a complete surprise when Bishop Alan Clark

The future of Norwich's only Roman Catholic church within the old city walls — St. George's Chapel in Fishergate – may soon be decided.

The flint building, which was closed last August when a wall collapsed, was left with its fate hanging in the balance as ways of saving it were examined.

Now, on application for redevelopment of the site for light industry — which already surrounds the chapel — has been submitted to the city council.

"We are still at the investigative stage," said Father Robert Manley, parish priest. "Depending on the response from the council, the land may be offered for lease or sale."

Another wall had been found to be leaning badly, and the cost of rebuilding would be great.

People were moving out of the centre of Norwich, said Father Manley.

"It seemed to us that because of the vast expense that would be involved in rebuilding the chapel, it was not a proposition we could take on," he explained.

"Part of our Catholic history has gone," he added.

The congregation had been distributed among other city churches, said Father Manley, and communion was taken to the elderly in their homes.

Mr. Geoffrey Lane, designing conservation group leader for Norwich City Council said: "It is not a listed building, or an historic one."

He confirmed that the chapel was "beyond economic repair — a write-off."

The ever popular Luncheon Club

asked me to come. Two things struck me immediately about the parish which was very welcoming and very active. The first was that it had no Catholic schools within its boundaries (and indeed still hasn't) and the second was that since the beginning of the parish in the 1890s, there had never been a resident religious community. So, I asked the then provincial of the IBVM sisters (now the Congregation of Jesus), Sister Francis North, whether they would consider establishing a foundation in the parish. A reply didn't come for about a year, but when it did, the answer was 'Yes'. And so Constitution Hill became, within a very short space of time, quite a hub within the parish. A community of four came, with Sisters Patricia and Colette engaged in parish catechesis and prison ministry, Sister Clem as the cook and parish visitor and the formidable Sister Margaret Mary, operating out of her comfort zone as a teacher, becoming active in the choir, the prayer group and in counseling. Very quickly she established a close friendship with a great characters of those days at St. George's, Paul Jarvis, one of the driving forces behind Turniptop which helped pay for the church. Paul was a gifted cartoonist, with a keen eye for the absurd, as can be seen in his creation, drawn after the bishop had made a reference to his need for priests.

Extraordinary Certificate of VISITATION
St. George's Norwich, 1984

'A bishop without priests is a bishop without arms and legs and, in this case, a head!' Bishop Alan Clark, 25 March 1984

Fr. Tony Rogers recalls that:

> Margaret Mary, with her very persuasive tactics, managed to find in Paul, both a confidant and a chauffeur, his little Mini, clocking up thousands of miles with cross-country dashes to various IBVM establishments up and down the land. Sad though it was that, out of necessity, the CJs had to close the convent on Constitution Hill, it is surely good news that Sister Mary Richard continues to live in the parish and continue the great work they began in 1984.[4]

Brenda Bailey reminds us of a beautiful and poignant feature of the church. She wrote:

> After the re-ordering of the Church in 1986 Fr. Tony Rogers asked Beryl Tuffs to organise the making of some kneelers for the weekday mass chapel. It was planned to have a kneeler representing every organisation in the parish, and the work began under Beryl's guidance in January 1987. Sadly Beryl became ill and died within a year, but we managed to finish all the kneelers in time for them to be blessed by Fr. Tony at a memorial Mass for her first anniversary. They are still being used in the Robert Southwell Chapel.[5]

Margaret Hanley, took over responsibility for the Lunch Club and rejuvenated its operations by strengthening the active team of cooks. Fr. Tony Rogers and his Assistant Priests became regular guests to these luncheons much to the pleasure of the members and throughout this period membership was maintained between 35 and 40. The popularity of these lunches spread beyond the parish boundaries and a number of parishioners from St. John's Parish became members.

Some reflections by Mrs. Barbara Allcock help illustrate life in the parish in the 1980s. Barbara and her friends, Pat Lipscome, Barbara Doggett and Mr. and Mrs. Worthington were all actively involved in fundraising and the social activi-

After Fr. Manley's forced retirement through illness and Fr. Leeming's move to Cambridge, Fr. Tony Rogers was appointed Parish Priest

ties that went with it. What started in 1981 and lasted until 1990 was a period of very active involvement. Barbara recalls:

> Much of the activity was organized by members of the Life Group and involved mystery tours as well such as a Tuesday night journey out, ending up at the Three Horseshoes in Scottow and besides enjoyment it raised another £65 for "Life" funds. My diary for those years shows parish activities in most months such as; BBQ; bingo; social committee; market stall; afternoon tea; mystery tour; Life meeting; reader at mass; sponsored knit in; church council; fuschia night; concert; bazaar. For one BBQ there was a turn out of over 80 supported by families such as: Davies, Kersey, Allcock, Fitzmaurice, Cushing, Webber, Lee, Richardson, Coe, Wick, Mann, Belling, Staniland, Harbor, Thompson, Callas and Kiernan.[6]

This little piece illustrates the parish in action. It's not just the people who come to the churches for their worship, it's about small and large groups coming together at various times to enact their faith together, to enjoy life, support each other and engage in activities that support the Church's mission. Another very important and popular aspect of parish life was the series of pilgrimages organised and led by the clergy at the time.

28 May/4 June 1988: Parish Pilgrimage to Assisi, The Vatican and Monte Cassino, led by Fr. Eugene Harkness (Assistant Priest St. George's) with 41 pilgrims.
26 May/3 June 1989: Parish Pilgrimage to Lourdes, led by Fr. Tony Rogers with 35 pilgrims.
June 1990: Parish Pilgrimage to Oberammagau, led by Fr. Philip Shryane with 30+ pilgrims.
May/June 1994: Parish Pilgrimage to Knock, led by Fr. Philip Shryane with 40+

Fr. Eugene Harkness led the 1988 pilgrimage to St. Peter's Rome

Fr. Philip Shryane led the parish from 1990 to the new millennium. He was an active supporter of our many pilgrimages during that time

pilgrims.

October / November 1997: Parish Pilgrimage to The Holy Land led by Fr. Philip Shryane with 40+ pilgrims.

June 1997 saw a wonderful flower festival to commemorate 25 years of the Norwich Life Group took place with 50 magnificent displays. Such festivals have been a regular beautiful and successful part of the parish life for many years.

1999: Parish Pilgrimage to Portugal and Santiago de Compostela, led by Fr. Shryane with 40 pilgrims.

Barbara Allcock remembered her good friend Cecily Green, who died on 10 December 1998:

Cecily was a parishioner at Our Lady's in Thorpe, she was an active member of the parish and deeply involved in social and fund raising activities. Cecily attended pottery evening classes at Thorpe St. Andrew High School and as her friends say – she excelled and her gifts were contributed to the parish in a very tangible way through the statue of St. Joseph at Our Lady's Church and the Stations of the Cross as well.[7]

CHAPTER 6

St. George's Today

As with all parishes the spiritual leadership of the parish is provided by the parish priest and St. George's, as our story has shown, has been blessed by having a succession of hard working men dedicated to the church and in supporting the parish community through its struggles and successes. The first decade or so of the new millennium was under the guidance of Fr. Tony McSweeney who was succeeded by Fr, Sean Connolly our current and highly respected parish priest. Fr. Sean was formally inducted as parish priest in 2015 and he provides a strong evangelising lead to the parish. Some of that outward facing spirit in the parish is captured by the contributions in this final chapter.

Parishes have always developed a broad range of clubs and societies to draw the people of the parish together and to help in living our mission. Over the last fifty years, however, we have seen some significant changes in the way different people have risen to the challenge of supporting our priests in running the parish at many different levels.

The church frequently faces the challenge of finding, training and keeping enough priests in every parish. The development of a greater role for deacons has been one very noticeable change in the spiritual leadership for our community. The current deacons are the Rev. Ian Hatfield and the Rev. Nick Greef. They are supported by the Sisters of the Congregation of Jesus who we have seen have been in the parish for over 30 years. They in turn are supported in our mission by a number of catechists, several of whom work wonders in helping our young people on their early journeys through the Blessed Sacraments.

This chapter illustrates some of the ways we live our vision as a community made up of many cultures and with a dedication to worshipping together, reaching out to the poor in our own area and to those in other parts of the world. The following short pieces show some of these important elements of a living, worshipping community, sometimes struggling but always trying to live our life in faith.

Looking to the wider world – our twinnings

The Diocese of East Anglia is twinned with Battambang, Cambodia and The Holy Land, Deacon Nick Greef reflects on some of the achievements:

> Bishop Michael suggested that St. George's parish should twin with a small rural parish community which consisted of two communities, these were a native Cambodian community in a small town called Pursat and a Vietnamese floating village community called Kompong Loung situated on a lake close to the town of Pursat. The parish priest is a Columbian Fr. Hernan Pinilla who also runs a crop science centre developing alternative crops to assist the local population. This twinning lasted for five years, from

Bishop Michael Evans encouraged parishes in the Diocese to partner overseas communities. St. George's is twinned with the Bethlehem Arab Society for Rehabilitation and, pictured, the Diocese of Battambang in Cambodia

2005 to 2010 and included a two-month visit to the communities by a parishioner, Dan Greef. Each year our parish sends Christmas cards to this and other parishes within both Cambodia and The Holy Land. The apostolic Prefect Kike Figaredo describes the effect of these Christmas cards as 'a shower of love descending across the communities'. Several fundraising events were organised during the period of twinning and a total of £6,000 was raised.

It was decided after five years to focus our fundraising within the Holy Land. Bishop Michael Evans suggested that we support a Catholic Hospital located in Bethlehem in the West Bank territory of Palestine. And so, since 2010 St. George's has supported the Bethlehem Hospital in the Holy Land managed by the Bethlehem Arab Society for Rehabilitation (BASR). 17 BASR was founded in 1960 as one of Leonard Cheshire's homes. BASR is a non-profit, non-government organisation that is nationally recognised for the comprehensive medical and rehabilitation services it renders to beneficiaries from different parts of Palestine, particularly those with disabilities regardless of their gender, age, religion or social class. BASR has worked progressively on its commitment to enhance the overall quality of life of persons with disabilities and other vulnerable groups, inspired by its mission for their total inclusion into all aspects of community life.

St. George's Parish organised a pilgrimage to the Holy Land in October 2011 when 25 parishioners visited the hospital and were met by the director and witnessed, first-hand, the work that the hospital does. We presented the hospital with an Icon of St. George as a gift of our twinning.[1]

The importance of music in the parish life and worship

In celebrating our faith, music plays a very big part in our worship and in the parish, another big change compared with 50 years or so ago when music was important but not something everyone could participate in. Paul Allen, the organist at St. George's and our musical leader, reflects on the development of music in the parish and his own journey:

I have been so very fortunate to have presided at the organ of St. George's for 35 years! The musical changes in that period have been immense. Firstly, we are all indebted to Geoffrey Laycock, who was the first organist at Sprowston Road. At the time he was director of music at Keswick Hall College. I am personally indebted to Geoffrey because he was very accommodating, allowing me to spend many hours practising in the church. If it had not been for him I am pretty sure that I would not have had the opportunity to play the organ at all. Some parishioners might, therefore, be cursing him by now!

It was Fr. Roy Gathercole who first asked me to play for the 11.00 Mass, which was in those days sung in Latin. The choir was singing at the earlier 9.15 Mass under the direction of Ray Howlings. I shared the playing with another parishioner, John Cracknell. As time moved on I found myself elevated to playing for the main Sunday mass and working with Ray and the choir.

The biggest occasion of all was the TV Mass in 1983. Concelebrating that were Fr. Tony Rogers, Fr. Gary Cawthorne & Fr. Simon Talbott. I remember first hearing about it early in the year and turning up for a practice on a very cold and snowy evening. What I had not been told was that Fr. Gary had composed a new Gloria for the occasion, so, you can imagine my slight horror to realise that it would be live on TV and I had never seen it before. Those of you that were there will remember it all went very well and, again, I still have the copy tape of it.

Over the years I have got used to adapting to new Mass settings and some new hymns, some much better than others! It has also been my pleasure to play for a fair number of weddings, taking this role on much later as I didn't feel competent enough to play some of the music.

When Ray became an ordained minister I approached Pete Cleary to take on the challenge of choral conductor and thankfully he agreed. Over the many years we have worked together we continue to strive to provide the best standards that we can, and

Paul Allen with the
new church organ

are always looking to find new music for the mass as well as new choral works to
enhance the services and, of course, we are always on the look out for more singers to
help us with our mission of music and song.

Funerals, too numerous to mention, have also kept me busy but the most memorable
have been that of Fr. Bob Manley, Fr. John Drew and Fr. Bernard Nesden. All lovely
priests to have worked with and much remembered.

I cannot finish without saying how thrilled I was when asked to plan for the new organ
after the Parish finance group and Fr. Tony agreed that the old one needed to be
replaced. I cannot express enough my thanks to them all for their vision and support.
I believe that we now have an instrument worthy of the building, and many far more
illustrious than me, have agreed with this sentiment. It will prove to be a good organ
for many years to come to support the worship of the Parish. [2]

Celebrating together is at the heart of our Parish and we enjoy our rich and varied
cultural mix with parishioners from very many countries around the world. One
of the other big changes in Parish life in the last forty years has been the role taken
on by the many Ministers of the Eucharist and Ministers of the Word. When St.
George's Church opened in the 1960's it would have been unheard of for lay
people to play any up front role in the church especially during services and especially during Mass. Now there is a thriving group of lay people who support the
parish in these ways as well as Ministers of the welcome, those who clean and
care for our churches and those who make sure that our flowers, music, and other
gatherings are well organised, well supported and add to our ability to worship.
   Kavitha Prakash, a new parishioner, at the time of writing reflects on becoming

The Church today, a busy, warm and friendly community

part of the parish:

> The first time I visited St. George's Parish was on Ash Wednesday 2011. At the end of the service, while we, (my husband, young daughter and myself) were waiting outside the church to introduce ourselves to the then Parish Priest when we met Charles Carver. He is a very religious, kind-hearted person who became our window to the community and gave us the insights we needed.
>
> In the following weeks I found that the parish community of St. George's is very warm, friendly and welcoming to people from different parts of the world and from diverse cultures. Initially we were not sure how we would be accepted, however, people were very forthcoming and made us feel so comfortable that I felt I needed to give something back by joining the Ministry of the Word in the parish. On the early days I was doing the readings many parishioners would come up at the end of Mass, and give me their compliments, and so did the parish priest. This encouragement made me feel really warm and welcomed and helped me integrate into the community at St. George's fully.
>
> There is always a sense of togetherness, kindness and generosity at St. George's. Everyone appreciates and makes the extra effort to make sure people who are new integrate quickly and bring out the best in them. For me, it made me feel at home in a place far away from my original home, and for this I thank the people who make up the parish community at St. George's. [3]

The changing nature of our society and the welcome the church gives to its world family has always meant that our parish is well represented by members from many different countries and backgrounds. Some nationalities have traditionally been well represented in our parish. The Irish from the nineteenth century and well into the late twentieth century. The Spanish, Italian and other West European migrants especially between the First and Second World Wars in the immediate aftermath as Europe re-settled after the devastation of war. Then in the 1950s and into the late twentieth century we welcomed parishioners from the West Indies, Africa and across Asia. The richness of our cultural backgrounds comes together in all its wonderful diversity in the togetherness of our parish. This is especially beautiful at times in the year when our bidding prayers are read out by members of the parish from around the world, at the last count I remember the prayers being in fifteen different languages.

A rich and varied community
Dr. Nadhim Shamoon a local teacher and member of the parish provides a great insight into the hundreds of personal stories that go to making up our rich and varied community:

> Moving over 3000 miles to a foreign country is never an easy decision or a choice made half-heartedly. However, in pursuit of my studies for a PhD from the University of East Anglia my wife and I made the move from Iraq to Norwich in 1986. In 1990 I was appointed as a Senior Scientific Researcher at the School of Environmental Sciences.
>
> Being away from our friends and family we were able nonetheless to take comfort within the local diocese. Originating from Iraq there are currently an estimated 1.5 million Chaldean Catholics worldwide who to this very day face wide spread perse-cution particularly in the Middle East. Furthermore there is also a real danger that the 3125 year old ancient language of Aramaic, spoken by Jesus will soon be extinct along with dwindling numbers of Chaldean Catholics. As Chaldean Christians our Chaldean Church united with the Catholic Church in the 16th Century and so made perfect sense to attend Mass at St. George's.
>
> Having settled in Norwich our three boys attended St. John's, St. Thomas More and Notre Dame Catholic Schools and I have no doubt played a key role in forming the young men they are today. We truly take comfort in being part of our local Church community, one small cog in the big wheel of more than 1 Billion Catholics that share our beliefs.[4]

A core value for our parish is reaching out to the poor. The Church's mission to look after those in need at home is captured through this short piece about the St. Vincent De Paul (SVP):

> During this period the SVP retiring collections have been reduced to two special collections each year, one around the feast of St. Vincent de Paul in September and the other on Maundy Thursday. Thanks to the generosity of our parishioners on these two

Fundraising with marmalade –
a vital source of funds for fragile
communities

occasions and to the weekly member's collections, the Conference managed to survive for most of each year without undue strain. Financial support from district and central councils can be arranged when necessary but very rarely has this been necessary. At the time of 'going to press' conference members remain at 12 which provides all the help needed to deal with the cases brought to the attention of the President.[5]

The Church's mission to look after those in need overseas is captured through this piece taken from the *Norwich Evening News* in November 2014 (though the story went nationwide) about our fantastic CAFOD fundraisers and supporters:

5000 Jars and counting – meet Norwich's 'marmalady' fundraiser
A Thorpe Hamlet grandmother has making marmalade down to a fine art after cooking up more than 5,000 jars to raise £10,000 to help people all around the world.

Gloria Irons' marmalade has even been taken to far-flung destinations such as Rwanda and Ethiopia for the locals to enjoy. The 70-year-old, from the city side of Harvey Lane, has been giving the marmalade away in return for donations to the Catholic Agency for Overseas Development (CAFOD) for the past 16 years, and says she plans to continue for as long as she is able.

Even breaking her wrist did not stop the grandmother-of-five, as she roped in her supportive husband Colin and supervised the marmalade making. She said: 'I can make 24 jars in two hours now, including washing and sterilising the jars. It got a bit tricky when I broke my wrist, but my husband Colin helped me.'

Mrs Irons, a retired carer, said: 'It all started by accident. I was going to a fete and I had forgotten to bake anything. I grabbed some jars of marmalade I had made and they sold like hot cakes. It just snowballed from there.' Her closely-guarded recipe for the orange variety proved an instant hit and began selling as quickly as she could make it.

Tea and cake,
dedication and
energy

A CAFOD worker took one jar to Rwanda, where Mrs. Iron's group of churches, St. George's in Sprowston Road, Our Lady Mother of God in Thorpe St. Andrew, and St. Boniface Church in Hellesdon, were supporting a community in Musha. She said: 'It was lovely to see the people with my marmalade in photos.'

Although the recipe changes slightly for Christmas punters, with some additional whisky in tinsel-decorated jars, there is another crucial ingredient. Mrs Irons said: 'I just put love into it. Through CAFOD, I have learnt a lot about the poverty in other countries. I want to help those less fortunate. They have so little and we have so much. We've raised money for different appeals over the years. One that sticks in my mind was the horrendous floods in Mozambique. We heard about a community who lived close to the river banks. 'Their homes were completely washed away. So, after the floods, CAFOD helped the community to build new homes, higher up the hills away from the river. I can remember this old boy sitting in his new tin hut. The icing on the cake for him was that he now had a tin roof. He said he felt like a king, and all he needed now was a wife. It's amazing to see that kind of sense of humour after all that had happened. It makes you feel quite humble.' [6]

Our churches provide a focal point for our worship but as said at the very beginning it is more than just the bricks and mortar. The parish is about the community working together, worshipping together and reaching out. So the final word in celebration of our parish community is to acknowledge the key part played by many members of the parish.

But involvement in the parish community is also noticeable in informal activities, social events and through the Catholic Women's League as well as the St. George's Ladies Guild, CAFOD, various Ministries of the Eucharist, The Word of Welcome, catechists, the choir, organists, flower arrangers, Scout and Guide leaders and of course our dedicated altar servers. This brief journey through our Parish story has tried to show how our current place and our current freedom to worship has been built on the very long traditions of our Church. From the earliest missionaries, through the gradual and sometimes bloody development of those freedoms and through difficult periods of our national and local history. Then with the dedication and energy of great men and women we had the foundations of our parish laid.

We have seen that the parish has been through many ups and downs, great periods of energy and development and periods also of difficulty. But the story to me is one of an energetic, hard working, proud community that has fought long and hard to establish its right to be a separate parish, to build and maintain three churches, to live with all the doubts and challenges that our forebears dealt with too. We are now in a time of great technological and social change. A time of great challenges to authority, to the role of the clergy, to commitment to organisations of any kind. A time when we need our faith and sense of community to support the next stages of our story.

It was Isaac Newton who said he made his discoveries by standing on the shoulders of the giants who came before him. I hope that by illuminating our story through this little book we can gather the strength of parish community and rekindle the values and energies of our forebears, our own giants so evident in the key chapters of our story.

Finally as you enter or leave St. George's take a glance above the outside doors. A sandstone plaque is in placed here which comes from the original St. George's known simply as 'Fishergate'. This was discovered abandoned under a pile of rubbish and debris in 2005. It is now in the same place in the new St. George's as it was in the old: a nice link with the past that cements this lovely church with its historic predecessor.

An historic link with our past: the cross from
Fishergate at the 'new' St. George's

Notes

Introduction
1 Michel Quoist – *Prayers of Life*, Logos Books 1971

Chapter 2
1 http://vatican2voice.org
2 *EDP* Thursday 19 March 1964.

Chapter 3
1 Maddermarket Theatre Norwich – brochure.
2 www.norfolkchurches.co.uk/norwichcatholic/norwichcatholic.htm
3 'A Gentle Salute to his charges against the Catholic Church', Rev. J Holden 1829 (Norfolk Archive Centre).
4 JJ McLean 'A Fine City, Fit For Heroes? The Rise of Municipal Housing in Norwich, 1900-1939 An Historical Perspective' www.heritagecity.org/user_files/downloads/housing-a-fine-city.pdf
5 The Valori family photos with thanks to Eva (daughter of Guido) still a parishioner at St. George's and Our Lady's in 2015.
6 Matthew Rowell online at www.thenorwichflood1912.com
7 *EDP* August 1912.
8 http://archive.thetablet.co.uk/article/10th-august-1912/12/the-national-catholic-congress
9 *Eastern Evening News* (*EEN*)of August 10 1912, 'An English Churchman of Norwich'.
10 JJ McLean 'A Fine City, Fit For Heroes? The Rise of Municipal Housing in Norwich, 1900-1939 An Historical Perspective'
www.heritagecity.org/user_files/downloads/housing-a-fine-city.pdf
11 Brundall Gardens in the 1920s-30s – the restaurant was run for many years by the Valori family.
12 Early memories of St. George's by Miss D Miller, Mrs. P Twomey, Miss P Delahan and Mrs L Hardy (1984).
13 Melinda Warrington of Thorpe St. Andrew (written note in October 2012).
14 Catherine Middleton (age 93) baptized at St. George's Fishergate in 1919 when interviewed at home in 2012.
15 Early memories of St. George's by Miss D Miller, Mrs. P Twomey, Miss P Delahan and Mrs L Hardy, 1984.
16 *Liber Matrimoniorum* St. George's Church Norwich.
17 St. George's *Parish Diary*.
18 *EEN*, March 1947.

Chapter 4
1 www.eafa.org.uk/catalogue/6203.
2 *East Anglian Guild Magazine* dated April 1950.
3 *The Northampton Diocesan Magazine* Spring 1951.
4 *Catholic Herald*, 20 July 1951.
5 Melinda Warrington of Thorpe St. Andrew (written in October 2012).
6 Melinda Warrington of Thorpe St. Andrew (written in October 2012).
7 Extracts from the *EDP* between 1970 and 1972.
8 *Catholic Herald*, 12 October 1973.

Chapter 5

1 Mike Howlings, interviewed and notes provided at the end of 2012.

2 Ibid.

3 Ibid.

4 Written note to the author by Fr. Tony Rogers in 2013.

5 Written note to the author by Brenda Bailey October 2015.

6 Written note to the author by Barbara Allcock in 2014.

7 Written note to the author by Barbara Allcock in 2014.

Chapter 6

1 Written note to the author by Nick Greef in 2013.

2 Written note to the author by Paul Allen in 2013.

3 Written note to the author by Kavitha Prakash in 2013.

4 Written note to the author by Nadhim Shamoon in 2013.

5 Mike Howlings, interviewed and notes provided at the end of 2012.

6 *Norwich Evening News* 20 November 2014.

ACKNOWLEDGEMENTS

Fr. Tony McSweeney for the original idea and persuading me to see if there was a story worth telling. Deacons Nick Greef and Ian Hatfield for their support and interest and contributions, Paul Allen our own parish music man – for his interest, insight and music, Jim Marshall for links to publishers.

Tessa who helped me access the files and books in the presbytery, chased people for me and always showed an interest in my little stories. Mike Howlings who provided invaluable extracts about Parish life over the last half century.

The parishioners who had a go at the history in the 1980s and whose file and notes were found in a box in the presbytery. Norfolk churches websites which provide a rich vein of comment and enquiry. George Plunkett's photographs by kind permission of his family – worth exploring online to see a wealth of images of Norfolk over the last half century or so. Several parishioners in 2012 / 2013 who gave of their time and encouragement including:

Ian Brundell; Melinda Warrington; Catherine Middleton; Veronica Short; Brenda Bailey; Frances Taylor, Mr William Howard and his wife Diane; Barbara and Terry Alcock; Kavitha Prakesh; Dr Nadhim Shamoon; Ralph and Jean Daynes; several members of the clergy with links past and present to St. George's especially those who submitted photographs or memories including: Fr. Bosco Clarke, Rev. Anthony Foreman, Fr. Tony Rogers and especially to those priests who kept a Parish diary from 1941 to 1960 which included various newspaper clippings that gave an insight into church matters.

Fr. David Jennings and Fr. Tony Rogers read drafts of the book for me to ensure there weren't any terrible theological blunders.

Finally to Fr. Sean Connolly whose interest and guidance and good sense about structure and the story has enabled this work to be finished.

A special thanks to those who read and amended my meanaderings, especially Diana Conney, Fr. Tony Rogers and Stephen Morris, whose editing and creative flair turned my research into a book others can enjoy. However, I accept full responsibility for errors that the eagle-eyed will continue to find.

'Yesterday, Today, For Ever'
a beautiful glass screen for the millennium